The Interdisciplinary Curriculum

Arthur K. Ellis
Carol J. Stuen

EYE ON EDUCATION
6 Depot Way West, Suite 106
Larchmont, N.Y. 10538

ISBN 1-883001-55-2

Library of Congress Cataloging-in-Publication Data

Ellis, Arthur K.
The interdisciplinary curriculum / by Arthur K. Ellis and Carol J. Stuen.
p. cm.
Includes bibliographical references (p.).
ISBN 1-883001-55-2
1. Curriculum planning--United States--Case studies.
2. Interdisciplinary approach in education--United States--Case studies. 3. Middle schools--United States--Curricula--Case studies.
4. Education, Secondary--United States--Curricula--Case studies.
I. Stuen, Carol J., 1951- II. Title.
LB1628.5.E55 1998
375'.001--dc21 98-5007
CIP

Production services provided by:
Bookwrights
1211 Courtland Drive
Raleigh, NC 27604

To Richard Scheuerman

Also available from Eye On Education

TEACHING IN THE BLOCK: STRATEGIES FOR ENGAGING ACTIVE LEARNERS
By Robert Lynn Canady and Michael Rettig

A COLLECTION OF PERFORMANCE TASKS AND RUBRICS: MIDDLE SCHOOL MATHEMATICS
By Charlotte Danielson

A COLLECTION OF PERFORMANCE TASKS AND RUBRICS: HIGH SCHOOL MATHEMATICS
By Charlotte Danielson and Elizabeth Marquez

HANDBOOK OF EDUCATIONAL TERMS AND APPLICATIONS
By Arthur Ellis and Jeffrey Fouts

RESEARCH ON EDUCATIONAL INNOVATIONS 2/E
By Arthur Ellis and Jeffrey Fouts

RESEARCH ON SCHOOL RESTRUCTURING
By Arthur Ellis and Jeffrey Fouts

PERFORMANCE ASSESSMENT AND STANDARDS-BASED CURRICULA
By Allan Glatthorn, with Don Bragaw,
Karen Dawkins, and John Parker

THE PERFORMANCE ASSESSMENT HANDBOOK
Volume 1, Portfolios and Socratic Seminars
By Bil Johnson

THE PERFORMANCE ASSESSMENT HANDBOOK
Volume 2, Performances and Exhibitions
By Bil Johnson

INSTRUCTION AND THE LEARNING ENVIRONMENT
By James Keefe and John Jenkins

THE EDUCATOR'S BRIEF GUIDE TO THE INTERNET AND WORLD WIDE WEB
By Eugene F. Provenzo, Jr.

Acknowledgments

We would like to thank the following people for giving us permission to share their experiences with a wider audience and for granting permission to reproduce their materials.

Butch Beedle	J.C. McKenna Middle School
Frederic Wilson Jill Adams	Huntingdon Area Middle School
Steven Cyr Mark Souza	Bartlett Middle School
Helen Bridges Rhonda Franke	North Kansas City High School
Linda DeBusk	Parkview High School
Kathy Coccetti Linda Fiorella Diane Marino	Horizon High School
Mary Godwin-Austen	Hidden Creek Elementary School

We would also like to thank Tom Maksym of Prentice-Hall's School Division.

PREFACE

All things are connected. —Chief Seattle

We have attempted to write this book in such a way that the reader can clearly make the connections between theory and practice in interdisciplinary teaching and learning. Critics have noted that interdisciplinary efforts are often, in fact, nondisciplinary in that they have little academic rigor, tending to be projects that do not bring out the depth of knowledge and skills found in the various disciplines. We think this is so because of a failure to connect theory in the form of powerful ideas and content to the day-to-day activities in which students are engaged. Our experience tells us that teachers are, in fact, desirous of using theories of learning and teaching in their practice. This book shows how it can be done.

To accomplish this goal, we have provided chapters that explain such necessary components of the process as inquiry and discovery, the nature of knowledge, concept formation, and reflective thinking. We also address such issues as integration of subject matter and academic integrity, the importance of major themes, and the crucial role of experience in learning. We connect these to such procedures as how to develop a successful thematic unit; connecting themes to outcomes; the application of constructivist ideas in the classroom; the use of cooperative learning strategies; group investigation, and how to make projects meaningful.

Finally, we offer classroom-tested examples and models of interdisciplinary curriculum. Teachers and administrators around the country are trying out some rather innovative and challenging things in the name of interdisciplinary curriculum, and we have attempted to offer the reader a sampler of best practice. The experience that comes from field testing can inform the reader about such practical questions as "What is a reasonable time frame for an interdisciplinary unit?" "How do I assess this kind of learning?" "What kinds of activities work best?" and "How is scheduling best arranged for this approach?"

Nothing is as powerful as an idea whose time has come. The idea of interdisciplinary teaching and learning has been around for many years, but now advances in learning theory, block scheduling, teacher interest, and the emerging arguments for linking theory and practice have given it the respect and momentum it deserves.

TABLE OF CONTENTS

1 The Knowledge Explosion and Academic Integrity 1
The Knowledge Explosion 3
Overflow of Information 4
Selective Coverage 6
Application of Knowledge 7
Fragmented Learning 8
Limitations of the Interdisciplinary Approach to Curriculum 10
The Interdisciplinary Experience and Preservation of Academic Integrity 12
The Spiral Curriculum 14
Progressive Roots 15
The Research Base for the Interdisciplinary Curriculum 18
The Research Agenda for the Future 21
Conclusion 21
References 25

2 From Teaching to Learning 27
The Discovery Experience 29
Curriculum as a Disciplinary Construct 30
Single Disciplinary Approach 32
Interdisciplinary Curriculum 35
Integration of Subject Matter 36
Integration of Teachers 37
Integration of Students and Community 37
The Teaching/Learning Process 38
Essence of Discovery 39
Preparation 39
Incubation 41

Illumination 42
Verification 43
Inquiry and the Journeys of Discovery 44
Shift in Emphasis 47
Making the Transition 48
References 55

3 Approaches to an Interdisciplinary Curriculum 57
The Project Approach 59
Why Use a Project Approach to the Curriculum 61
Application of Knowledge 61
Consideration of Students' Interests 62
Making School-to-Life Connections 62
Addressing the Information Revolution 63
Integration of Subject Areas 63
Considerations in Designing a Successful Project 64
Selection of a Topic, Problem, or Question 64
The Interdisciplinary/Collaborative Nature of the Project 66
The Structure of the Project 66
Adequacy of Resources 67
Collection of Data 67
Astronomy and the Project Approach 68
Conclusion 69
Using Themes in an Interdisciplinary Curriculum 69
Developing a Successful Theme Unit 71
Choosing a Theme of Study 71
Writing Outcomes 72
Connecting the Theme to the Outcomes 73
Selecting Activities 75
Assessment of the Unit 77
Team Teaching 77
Why the Decision to Team Teach? 80
How Does Teaming Work? 81
Cooperative Learning 82

Cooperative Learning Methods:
Group Investigation 83
Stages of Group Investigation 84
Conclusion 86
References 87

4 Interdisciplinary Curriculum in the School: What Teachers Are Doing 89
Rain Forests and Social Responsibility. Sixth Grade 93
STREAMS: Science Teams in Rural Environments for Aquatic Management Studies. Grades 5–8 106
Journeys of Discovery. Grades 5–8 116
Colonial Times and the Revolutionary War. Eighth Grade 125
Integrated Teaching and Learning: History and English. Ninth Grade 130
ABC's of Interdisciplinary Projects. Ninth Grade 137
Horizon High School: School-Wide Model of Interdisciplinary Teaching. Grades 9–12 139

5 Interdisciplinary Curricular Resources 143

6 Glossary 161

About the Authors

Arthur Ellis, the author of eleven published books and numerous journal articles, is Professor Of Education at Seattle Pacific University. Previously he taught in public school and at the University of Minnesota. He consults to various school systems in the United States and abroad. He is the co-author of an interdisciplinary curriculum on Lewis and Clark.

Carol Stuen is assistant Director of the International Center for Curriculum Studies in the School of Education at Seattle Pacific University, where she also teaches. She has done research on citizenship education both in the United States and in other countries, and has consulted with various schools districts.

1

The Knowledge Explosion and Academic Integrity

THE KNOWLEDGE EXPLOSION

Integrated studies are often cited as a useful way for teachers and students to make the necessary connections between and among the key ideas of the various academic disciplines. Advocates of integrated studies claim that the traditional curriculum model, which keeps academic subjects apart from one another, deprives learners of the opportunity to explore the relationships necessary to the development of deeper, fuller understanding of content. For example, integrationists claim that students studying life in frontier America in a history class would naturally benefit from a simultaneous, coordinated study of the literature, art, and science of that era. This makes perfect sense to those who wish to see the curriculum centered around broad themes that have multiple touch points; yet it rarely happens.

Oddly enough, the reason that it rarely happens in secondary schools has less to do with teacher resistance—although that factor should not be discounted—than with schedules, time blocks, and the sequestering of teachers in their respective academic departments of the school. It rarely happens in elementary schools for a related but different reason: textbooks dominate the curriculum, and textbooks written for different subjects at a particular grade level are neither coordinated nor otherwise related to one another. In either case, specialization of subject matter triumphs over integration. As a result, at both levels intellectual gaps separate the subjects, and students are left to their own devices to make any meaningful connections. Occasionally, an inspired teacher or team of teachers will try to bridge the gaps, and when they do, good things begin to happen. The advent of block scheduling has been one very positive step forward as a means of facilitating cooperation among teachers.

It is also claimed by advocates of integrated studies that for teachers to "cover" the amount of subject matter imbedded in each discipline has become increasingly difficult due to the exponential growth of knowledge in recent years. This fact of curricular life is given as a reason for seeking ways to combine subjects in a search for meaningful ways to reduce the redundancy which is inevitable in separate subject approaches. For example, germ theory is covered in both biology and health classes. Why not, integrationists ask, develop a thematic approach to germ theory that involves not only biology and health, but the history of scientific breakthroughs that led to different ideas about the spread and prevention of disease? It is argued that integrative themes can provide an economy of scale not available when teachers plan and teach their classes in isolation.

Thematic teaching also allows for the accommodation of new topics that are constantly emerging, such as AIDS education or environmental studies, without compromising the integrity of the subject matter from different disciplines. The extent to which it is reasonable to blend disciplines in order to make learning coherent, against the possibility that the essence of particular subjects might be lost in the process, is not a matter that has been subjected to very much empirical testing. Therefore, most of the claims for and against it lie in the realm of considered opinion.

All of this is somewhat problematic, of course, because the arguments on behalf of integrated studies are generally based on certain assumptions about the nature of knowledge. To the extent that teachers and others with a vested interest in the interdisciplinary curriculum think those arguments are persuasive, the assumptions make sense. Let us examine those assumptions. There are four such assumptions worthy of consideration.

OVERFLOW OF INFORMATION

The first assumption about the nature of knowledge is that there is simply too much information to contain it in a school curriculum. Let us cite a specific example. To take as our measure of the amount of information available from which one might build a curriculum, let us confine ourselves to one medium: print. If we were to define the print medium as all the books, periodicals, newspapers, papyrus scrolls, clay tablets, etc., ever produced, we could say, metaphorically, that from the dawn of time, when the first printing occurred (perhaps a sketch in charcoal on the wall of a cave), up to the year 1850, there was an accumulation of print deep enough to cover the earth to a depth of one inch. The year 1850 is Abraham Lincoln's time, Charles Dickens' time, Louis Pasteur's time.

Now something amazing happened in the next one hundred years, the time between 1850 and 1950, a time span that included the contributions to the knowledge base of Jane Austen, Albert Einstein, Ernest Hemingway. The amount of knowledge produced in the print medium during this time is said to have doubled. So by 1950, metaphorically, the earth was covered to a depth of two inches. In one century, as much print knowledge was produced as in all the preceding centuries combined. How does one build a meaningful school curriculum when the knowledge base has doubled in the space of a few generations? How does one know what to include, what to leave out, when there is twice as much information available? This is all quite vexing to people who take matters of curriculum seriously.

And in the years from 1950 to 1990 it is reckoned that the amount of print covering the earth increased to a depth of 36 inches. Furthermore, it is guessed that the year 2000 marks a depth of about 100 inches. Knowledge feeds on itself, resulting in geometric rather than linear expansions. Those devoted to complete coverage of subjects in the school curriculum will need to look elsewhere for comfort. There is simply too much to cover. And the overall expansion of knowledge can be applied to individual subjects.

Years ago a typical small town school library carried a then-impressive total of 30 or more periodicals, including weeklies and monthlies. There were more magazines there than one person could read, and that was the general idea. Today a typical supermarket carries 200 to 300 periodicals tucked away on shelves in a corner of the store. As well, a typical large city library offers its readers more than 3000 titles of periodicals from which to choose. No matter how you look at it, the amount of knowledge available from which to build curriculum is out of control. Traditional attempts at coverage won't work, and some means of combining subject matter is at least one answer to the dilemma. Hence, the case for integration.

But combining subjects even where it might make sense to do so is not enough. There is still too much to cover, especially when one considers that the mere combining of subjects offers no guarantee that the combinations arrived at will represent the essential knowledge from the various disciplines selected for integration.

SELECTIVE COVERAGE

This brings us to the second assumption about the nature of knowledge and integrated studies: selective coverage. Because integrated studies offerings are usually based on themes, they make no pretense about coverage in the traditional sense. Rather the approach is more often oriented toward large ideas that cut across disciplinary boundaries. Mortimer Adler's Great Books program, for example, is based on the writings of hundreds of authors over the centuries, and its focus is on important ideas that have changed the world. Those ideas include justice, power, love, wealth, beauty, etc. The point of the program is that if students are interested in how the idea of citizenship, for example, has been developed by great thinkers over time, they merely need to follow that theme in their studies. And because citizenship is truly a theme not restricted to any one academic discipline, the readings come from science, history, civics, literature, the arts, mathematics, philosophy, religion, economics, etc. As an aside, Adler's program provides a useful adjunct to integrated studies programs because it lends some of the needed intellectual perspective often lacking in activity-oriented integrated studies curricula.

But regardless of the proportional emphasis on a traditional or activity-oriented approach to teaching and learning, integrationists argue that the focus on significant ideas or themes offers a way out of the forest of information in which it is becoming increasingly easy to get lost. Thus integrated studies, or at least thematic learning, would appear to have an upper hand in this equation because, by definition, it should seek the best points of intersect among disciplines, and those points are invariably found in the realm of significant ideas. However, opponents will argue that the same procedure can be followed within specific academic disciplines, and that it is not an exclusive feature of integrated studies. Good teachers, it is claimed, have always taught this way, drawing out significant ideas and connecting them to larger patterns.

Application of Knowledge

The third assumption integrated studies makes about the nature of knowledge is that it should be learned for reasons that transcend the ordinary academic purposes of school life. What is essentially at stake here is the application of knowledge to real life experience. Anyone who has taken a course in foreign language or educational statistics knows how difficult it is to remember even the basics from the course. Even people who achieved top grades will say things like, "I don't remember much; I just studied for the tests." We should not be surprised that when teaching and learning is purely academic in the sense of "learn the material and show that you learned it on the test," students neither expect to retain what they studied, nor to use it in any practical way. This is not so much a way of saying that the knowledge was trivial in the first place, or even that such courses have no value. The reason for the atrophy may be that, for most learners, the opportunity to apply the information they "learned" never presented itself. Aristotle noted in his writing that it is in *doing* that we learn best. His point was that knowledge applied has more staying power. A common approach to learning in integrated studies is the project method. Projects are things you *do,* not just information you learn. Much of the current thought in brain research suggests that human beings are "wired" to do projects, that projects are a natural way for us to learn.

Such an approach to the curriculum and to knowledge inevitably takes students and teachers out into the real world. An example of such an interdisciplinary approach to knowledge is a project done recently by a group of middle school students at

James Bay Community School in Victoria, B.C. The students were responsible for the removal of all chlorofluorocarbon-containing styrofoam cups, etc., from the food services of the British Columbia Ferry System and from the Victoria Public Schools. Just imagine the amount of research in different areas that students would need to do in order to put together a project that resulted in such dramatic changes in public policy. Projects have a way of energizing learners with the power of knowledge applied. And to those who question whether all knowledge has direct application to the real world, my answer is no, just as my answer is no to the question of whether it is reasonable to attempt to integrate every facet of the curriculum. Such questions, however, are rather diversionary when one considers the lost opportunities to make real world applications and to integrate studies where it is reasonable to do so.

The most cogent counter argument to projects as a way to make knowledge meaningful is that school, by definition, is not the real world. It is purposely set aside from real life as a time to acquire the vast reservoirs of knowledge that separate us from other creatures. Attempts to carry out "real life" projects, it is said, destroy the very reason for having school in the first place. Projects are available to us throughout life, even during non-school hours during the school years, but the opportunity to study academic knowledge in disciplined settings occurs only during the school years.

FRAGMENTED LEARNING

Interdisciplinary curriculum means curriculum that combines and somehow integrates two or more typically separate disciplines. Obviously, in order to accomplish this some accommodations must be made. This is true because school subjects are typically taught in isolation in spite of all the talk about interdisciplinary approaches to teaching and learning. When a subject, say mathematics or English, is taught in isolation, that subject can be given complete attention by the teacher and students. The subject itself is the focus of attention. It becomes an end in itself rather than a means to some other end. On the other hand, when two or more subjects are combined, the focus changes, however subtly. More time is spent trying to explore and act on the possible relationships between the subjects. The relationship is often established by identifying a common theme to which each of the disciplines can make some meaningful contribution. Such a theme might be "Exploration," "Discovery," "Environment," etc. Thus the idea of the theme becomes the end and the contributing disciplines become means toward that end.

This is not to say that a given teacher teaching one subject might not attempt to relate that subject to other areas of life. But that is what we would call a random effect. One teacher tries to establish connections and another does not. When teachers consciously try to teach more than one subject together, the attempt to make connections, at least from one subject to another, is no longer a random, but a planned effect. This logic pertains for students as well depending on whether they study subjects apart or study them together.

Teachers, students, parents, and others who have something at stake in the educational enterprise must be convinced that the needed accommodations in the traditional structure of separately taught disciplines is worthwhile. This is not always an easy task, and the challenge of doing it well should not be underestimated. People have every right to question a break with the traditional, discipline-centered curriculum and its replacement with an interdisciplinary, thematically oriented approach to the curriculum. In fact, the arguments for keeping subjects separated are often compelling. It is important to keep in mind that not everything can or should be integrated. The judgments of what to integrate and what to leave to separate account are the judgments that teachers need to make wisely and with discernment. Just as it is often patently artificial to separate students' learning experiences into academic disciplines that may make sense to the advance scholar but not to the student, so too, there is a very real danger that accompanies the tyranny of forced integration.

What happens to learning when students are taught separate subjects, out of context with and related to one another? As we noted above, sometimes it is necessary to do so, but far more often the failure to integrate knowledge leads to a failure of the promise of a liberal education to become a reality. The purpose of the middle school is more about citizenship, participation, and a desire to learn than it is about the so-called mastery of separate subjects. It is during these years of emergence from childhood that students begin to glimpse the possibilities of scholarship, but more often their immediate interests run to friendships, projects, and activities.

These interests are frequently treated as problems that get in the way of learning. This is often the case to the extent that school learning consists, as John Goodlad has observed, mainly of teacher presentations and what is euphemistically called seatwork. This is not an argument for school merely as a place of social gathering or as a place where students do whatever they choose. Rather, it is an attempt to say that cooperative activities, group projects, and schools—as places where citizenship, participation, and espirit de corps are at the heart of the curriculum—are far more likely to ignite the spark of learning, than are the contrived, expert-oriented, narrow confines of separate subjects (which diminish not only academic connections but the connections among teachers as well). One of the great ironies of school life is that we expect students to put the various curricular pieces together into something called a liberal education when teachers themselves make no claim to having done it. We expect students to emerge from our schools with a sense of citizenship when the faculty itself seldom works together, which is the beginning of citizenship. A useful principle to keep in mind is that the logical consequence of the separation of faculty from one another and the deliberate separation of subjects from each other is a fragmented sense of knowledge and of self among learners. When teachers work in isolation, when subjects are taught in isolation, why should we not expect students to view learning as fragmented? And why should they themselves not feel isolated?

LIMITATIONS OF THE INTERDISCIPLINARY APPROACH TO CURRICULUM

The primary purpose of this book is to extol the virtues of the interdisciplinary approach to curriculum. But like anything else, no matter how beneficial, it can be both overdrawn and misapplied. The two potentially most damaging applications of interdisciplinary curriculum are (1) its siren call of superficiality, and (2) the temptation to use it when a separate subjects approach would better serve both teachers and students. Let us look at each of these problems in turn.

Among traditionalists and subject matter specialists there is great reluctance to abandon the teaching of important subjects separately. This is so because they fear that mathematics, literature, history, etc., will be watered down and treated superficially in an attempt to meet the compromising demands of some central theme around which an interdisciplinary unit is typically organized. There is the accompanying concern that the orderly progression of knowledge and skills taught when a subject is treated as a curriculum in and of itself will be lost in a random, patchwork attempt to relate it to the particular theme. Finally, what one is left with, the critics note, is a shallow, disorganized treatment of mathematics or literature, or whatever, lacking both depth and continuity. Thus the integrity of a typical mathematics concept such as "measurement" is sacrificed in order to meet the demands of a theme such as "community helpers." Or the beauty and symmetry of a poem such as "Paul Revere's Ride" is misused as an example of an interdisciplinary theme of "transportation." Because of the focus on the organizing theme in a typical interdisciplinary unit, a subject that could be treated in depth as an end in itself becomes merely a means to another end. When this is the case, the subject itself is susceptible to superficial, random treatment. The temptation to consider academic subjects from a purely utilitarian point of view (that is, how well they fit a particular theme) can lead to such disasters as lower test scores, lessened exposure to the possibilities of a particular subject, and the dominance of some curricular areas, such as social studies, over others, such as mathematics, etc.

The other related problem, that of doing interdisciplinary curriculum when a separate subjects approach might well be superior, is just as vexing. This is an issue that teachers must address carefully. The question should be tied to the curricular goal structure. What are the important things that students must study, and how should they study them? Of course, there is no predictable answer to such a question because local circumstances must always be taken into account. The important thing is not to assume the inherent superiority of one approach over another but to think through the implications for student learning. The answer to this question is to consider carefully the implications of combining subjects as opposed to keeping them apart. We should search for meaningful ways in which to integrate learning toward some sense of the seamless whole, but we should never assume that integration is the only answer. In other words, the burden of proof should lie with integration, and not the other way around.

The temptations to integrate subjects or to keep them separate can be avoided by answering a simple question: What is best for students? In other words, decisions made with reference not to an abstract policy which favors separation or integration of subject matter, but with reference to contextual matters such as the development of citizenship, morality, knowledge, skills, and self-realization, will be the best decisions. One can only conclude that sometimes the best answer is integration and sometimes it is separation of subject matter.

THE INTERDISCIPLINARY EXPERIENCE AND PRESERVATION OF ACADEMIC INTEGRITY

Let us turn our attention to a practical application of interdisciplinary curriculum and the question of preserving academic integrity. It is typically the case that interdisciplinary efforts are centered around an organizing theme. Any theme chosen by teachers and students must have sustaining value, and it must be rich in its potential to include the various academic disciplines as meaningful contributors. Thus the choice of themes must be based on some strategic vision of what students need to learn and the ways in which they might learn. In other words, a strategic vision is based not on some set of outcomes agreed to in advance on behalf of students, but upon the potential for a course of study to be complex in its possibilities for student choices, individual initiative, teacher and student collaboration, projects, and substantive meaning.

An example of such a theme is Exploration. Of course, there are many other themes equally rich in possibilities, but Exploration will do for purposes of illustration. We will take the position that interdisciplinary themes should be selected by teachers and not by students. This is so for two reasons. First of all, teachers themselves must be interested in a topic, and they must be convinced that it has the potential to provide a range of experiences that meaningfully incorporate the various contributing subject matter areas. This is not such a simple matter. But if teachers are not convinced of the contributory potential of a theme, they certainly will not be able to convince their students of its value. Secondly, as teachers we have a responsibility to make decisions about what knowledge is of most worth for the young while keeping in mind that most worthwhile knowledge contains a wide array of possible choices within it for student learning. Thus students are provided with a structure of agreed-upon content, while at the same time they are given the opportunity to find themselves within it. This is the strategic balance between anarchy and authoritarianism in a course of study. It is called democracy.

In the *Journeys of Discovery* curriculum (see Chapters 4 and 5) for middle school students, the idea of Exploration becomes not merely a vehicle for identifying meaningful content but a metaphor for the entire process of teaching and learning. The journeys of various explorers serve to personify the quest through the diaries and accounts of these explorers, thus giving the course of study a human scale which removes it from the abstract, coverage-centered accounts found in typical textbooks.

Once it is agreed that a theme has rich curricular potential, the next step is to seriously consider the possibilities for the various subject matter areas of the curriculum to contribute to the theme. This alone distinguishes interdisciplinary efforts from the separate subjects approach. This is so because teachers will have to collaborate, with each teacher taking the lead in showing how his/her discipline can best contribute. A kind of synergy flows from such deliberations, at least when things go well. Teachers will have to model cooperative efforts in order to move the planning stages forward. They will have to practice the same kinds of give and take that one hopes students themselves will experience when the curriculum is realized in classroom life. These experiences in themselves represent exploration in the finest sense of the word.

Obviously, a theme such as Exploration is filled with geographic and historical potential. But it quickly extends as well into literature in the form of narrative and epic accounts of adventure. Anyone interested in "exploring" the possibilities that the contributions mathematics might bring to the theme of Exploration discovers the applications of measurement, scale, distance, estimation (for example, Columbus' estimation of the earth's circumference was not nearly so accurate as that derived by those early geometers, the ancient Greeks), time, etc. The science curriculum offers the central skills of science, such as observing, recording, classifying, and verifying, in addition to the study of technological advances that have made continued exploration possible throughout the ages. Artistic and musical themes emerge as well. Themes such as Exploration are, in fact, so rich in academic curricular potential that the problem becomes not whether disciplines can contribute to the course of study, but how to parcel out the contributions from one grade level to the next in some useful sequence, a point we will consider next.

THE SPIRAL CURRICULUM

One of the more liberating ideas in the annals of curriculum development is the concept of the spiral curriculum. In essence, the spiral curriculum is based on the premise that it is crucial to identify those key concepts, skills, and values that students should experience and to teach them each year at increasing levels of sophistication. This allows teachers to choose a stable core of important ideas and to teach them every year while varying the content through which they come to life. Such a perception changes the curriculum experience from the false idea of mastery to the reality that learning is more a journey than a point of arrival. By changing the content of what is taught while retaining the core values, concepts, and skills, teachers give students the opportunity to visit and revisit life's important themes. This is the beginning of meaningful learning.

When a matrix of important concepts, skills, and values is established, a curriculum is less susceptible to randomness and the "jumping around" so often associated with interdisciplinary thematic teaching and learning. Thus a question that should be posed prior to the identification of topics and themes is, "What are the most important concepts, skills, and values that each subject matter area can contribute to student learning?" This question can and should be posed independent of the themes and topics chosen for study. It is the single best guarantee that the curriculum will not become frivolous, skipping superficially from one theme to the next, nor imbalanced in favor of one or two subject areas over others. These remain two of the most pressing criticisms of interdisciplinary curriculum, and often the criticisms are right on the mark.

PROGRESSIVE ROOTS

The primary theoretical basis of the interdisciplinary curriculum is found in progressive educational philosophy. The progressive movement, which included such luminaries as John Dewey, William Kilpatrick, George Counts, and Harold Rugg, reached its zenith earlier in this century. It is a learner-centered approach that places greater emphasis on creativity, activities, "naturalistic" learning, real-world outcomes, and above all, shared experience.

Progressive education came to be known for what it opposed as much as for what it advocated. This was a matter of great concern to Dewey and others. Progressives were opposed to the factory-like efficiency model on which schools depended (and still do). They decried the artificial instruction and learning driven by textbooks and written exams. They said that school learning was so unlike the real world that it had little or no meaning to the average child. Robert Hutchins, not a progressive, said it best: "Students resort to the extra-curriculum because the curriculum is so stupid".

In his classic work, *Interest and Effort in Education*, Dewey wrote eloquently, establishing the thesis of progressivism and therefore of interdisciplinary studies:

> Our whole policy of compulsory education rises or falls with our ability to make school life an interesting and absorbing experience to the child. In one sense there is no such thing as compulsory education. We can have

> compulsory physical attendance; but education comes only through willing attention to and participation in school activities. It follows that the teacher must select these activities with reference to the child's interests, powers, and capacities. In no other way can she guarantee that the child will be present. (Dewey, 1913, p.ix)

The other, more recent theoretical basis for interdisciplinary curriculum is found in constructivist theory. The constructivity principle states that "activity should always precede analysis." Put another way, this means that experience and reflection on experience is the key to meaningful learning—not someone else's experience abstracted and condensed into textbook form, but one's own direct experience. Analysis, or reflective thought, should then follow the experience. In this sense, the traditional curriculum is not merely turned around, it is stood on its head.

Constructivist theory can be traced in part to the ideas and work of Lev Vygotsky, a Russian psychologist who was interested in child growth and development. He proposed a framework for understanding how children learn, focusing specifically on the relationship between language and cognitive development. His ideas received little attention in the West until the publication in 1962 of his book, *Thought and Language.* Vygotsky presented four main ideas for consideration. These included the belief that:

- children construct knowledge
- cognitive development is tied to social interactions
- learning can lead development, and
- language plays a central role in cognitive development.

Like Jean Piaget, Vygotsky believed that learners construct their own knowledge. Unlike Piaget, however, he suggested that this construction takes place not just through interaction with physical objects but through social interactions. That is, cognitive development is "socially mediated." It is the social interaction related to hands-on manipulation of objects that allows learners to construct knowledge. Shared experience necessarily involves language, which is central to the Vygotskian framework. Language, he proposed, impacts not only the development of cognition-what we know-but also has a vital role in the *process* of cognition-how we acquire knowledge.

Vygotsky discussed one other concept related to the way children learn. It is his contention that development and learning could be conceptualized in terms of the Zone of Proximal Development (ZPD). This zone, or continuum of behaviors, extends, on the one end, from the knowledge and skills that a child demonstrates independently to those at the other end that the child performs with assistance. Between these two extremes are performances that can be accomplished "partially-assisted." A child's behaviors, skills, and knowledge are constantly changing within the ZPD: what a child can do with assistance one day he or she may do independently the next. It is easy to see that the level of assisted performance changes as the child develops. It is the job of the teacher to provide experiences and interactions that challenge the child to move from assisted to independent performance, thereby advancing his or her cognitive development. Providing experiences at the lower end of the ZPD, where independence has already been achieved, will prove to be boring for the child, while offering experiences beyond the level of assisted performance will leave the child frustrated and confused. For example, asking the child to perform single-digit addition problems when he or she has already mastered that skill will prove to be neither challenging nor motivating. However, moving from one-digit to two-digit addition problems involving the process of carrying will likely be too big a step, and will discourage the child. The teacher, then, is faced with the difficult task of determining what types of tasks are appropriate in this case in terms of the child's ZPD.

Constructivist teaching and learning, then, "challenges the long-standing societal view that knowledge and skill come in finished, polished pieces" and that the role of the teacher is to give those pieces intact to the student (Joyce & Weil, 1996, p. 50). Although the work done in constructivist thought is quite recent, it is essentially in harmony with the earlier thinking of the progressives.

Advocates of integrating the curriculum also cite pure research in the area of brain function. They point to research that indicates that the brain seeks pattern and that this is a basic process. They believe that the brain resists learning that is fragmented, personally meaningless and presented in isolation. Contrariwise, they note that knowledge is learned more quickly and remembered longer when constructed in a meaningful context in which connections between and among ideas are made.

But not everyone agrees. Thomas Sowell is particularly critical of interdisciplinary teaching and learning, calling it "another popular buzzword." He notes that much of what passes for interdisciplinary is in fact *nondisciplinary*, in that it simply ignores boundaries between disciplines. He states further that, "academic disciplines exist precisely because the human mind is inadequate to grasp things whole and spontaneously, or to judge 'the whole person'. Thus, mathematics must be separated out for special study, even though it is an ingredient in a vast spectrum of other activities" (Sowell, 1995, p. 205).

THE RESEARCH BASE FOR THE INTERDISCIPLINARY CURRICULUM

Researcher Kathy Lake (1994) examined the available research and concluded that there are "no detrimental effects on learning when students are involved in an integrated curriculum" (p. 7). She was able to locate a few studies dating as far back as 1965 to show that some students actually learned more in the integrated curriculum, and she noted some educational advantage, such as teacher cooperation. However, she was cautious about reaching conclusions regarding the benefits of integrated studies because of the limited amount of research.

Since Lake's summary of the research, at least one study of note has been reported. Morrow, Pressley, and Smith (1995) report the interesting results of a well-crafted study of the effects of integrating literacy and science programs. Their remarks indicate "clear support for integrating literacy and science instruction at the third-grade level with respect to the development of language arts competencies," which "did not come at a cost to science content learning" (p. 25). If advocates of integrating the curriculum wish to substantiate their enthusiastic claims with empirical data, additional studies will have to be conducted. At this stage, the number of empirical studies remains so small that any kind of meaningful meta-analysis that might point to some generalized findings is precluded.

"Humanitas," an interdisciplinary humanities program for secondary students, was evaluated in the Los Angeles Unified School District using what appears to be a very careful design (Aschbacher, 1991). The program evaluation, carried out by the Center for the Study of Evaluation at UCLA, could well serve as a model for this type of sorely needed research. Achievement comparisons of Humanitas students and students from comparison groups showed that the program had very positive effects on students' writing and history content knowledge during the first year, and the improvement continued as students stayed in the program, which they did in greater percentages than did their counterparts in four comparison schools. Other sophisticated aspects of the evaluation included surveys of the students, teacher, and administrators, observations in the classrooms, analyses of teacher' assignments and examinations, reviews of student portfolios, and an examination of such "educational indicators" as school attendance, discipline problems, and "college-oriented" behaviors by students. Classroom observation, for example, showed that Humanitas students spent more time per day in thoughtful discussions with a greater number of students participating than did comparison groups. And even though Humanitas students received assignments judged to be harder than those given to comparison group students, the Humanitas students liked school better than did comparison students. We recommend a careful reading of the evaluation study (Aschbacher and Herman, 1989) by personnel in any district interested in doing serious program evaluation.

Going back more than half a century, one encounters what is generally considered to be the most celebrated program evaluation study ever conducted. It was called "The Eight Year Study," sponsored by the Progressive Education Association, now defunct, but then still a force in education. The purpose of the Eight Year Study, begun in 1933 and reported in 1942, was to determine whether a curriculum designed to meet the "needs and interests" of students was as effective in preparing students for college as was a traditional, subject-centered program. The study involved 30 progressive or experimental high schools which were matched as closely as possible with traditional comparison schools. Much of the curricular experience in the progressive schools was interdisciplinary in nature. The results of the Eight Year Study indicated that students from the progressive schools were as well prepared for college as their traditional counterparts with regard to academics, and were more involved in such social and extracurricular activities as yearbook, student government, clubs, etc. In spite of the evidence, the many pressing issues of World War II obscured the results, and as Decker Walker writes, "the reforms of this period survived only in isolated places and as the seeds of further reforms" (Walker, 1990, p. 72).

We realize that it is stretching things a bit to claim the Eight Year Study as a program evaluation of interdisciplinary curricula. However, many of the curricular offerings in the progressive schools were what are called "core curriculum," which is a way of combining subjects, say English and history, into a single offering called "Social Living." In fact, much of middle school philosophy emerged from the progressive movement, and one of the middle school tenets is to coalesce subjects into integrated studies using block scheduling.

Finally, there are some emerging research findings that do support tangentially the use of an integrated curriculum. One source of such research is the updated effective schools findings. Effective schools research has been conducted for several decades, yielding a variety of lists of school characteristics that distinguish "more effective" schools from less effective ones. These characteristics are thought by some to have a cause and effect relationship with respect to learning. Such attributions can really only be considered hypotheses, yet to be tested empirically. Still, these characteristics do point toward possibilities of why some schools may be better than others. The most recent effective schools research (Cotton, 1995) identified the following among a long list of classroom and school attributes:

- Teachers provide instruction that integrates traditional school subjects, as appropriate.
- Teachers integrate workplace readiness skills into content-area instruction.

- Administrators and teachers integrate the curriculum, as appropriate.

A second body of research is emerging from the many restructuring efforts currently underway across the nation. Lee and Smith's study of 820 secondary schools led them to conclude that "the consistent pattern of findings allows us to make quite unequivocal statements about the organizational structure of high schools: students learn more in schools which are restructured . . ." (Lee & Smith, 1994a, p. 23), and about 25 percent of these restructured schools were using "interdisciplinary teaching teams" (Lee & Smith, 1994b).

We recognize the limitations inherent in any hard and fast attempts to apply this research to interdisciplinary teaching and learning. But the results reported in this chapter do give us a place to begin, a kind of port of entry to this intriguing landscape. What is needed now is a systematic way in which to enlarge both the quantity and quality of the findings derived from carefully crafted qualitative and quantitative research studies. Perhaps what it will take is the establishment of some sort of center for the study of interdisciplinary curriculum.

THE RESEARCH AGENDA FOR THE FUTURE

What more do we need to know about achievement results and interdisciplinary curriculum? The answer to that is, much more. The sound theoretical base for this approach does not necessarily guarantee positive results. The types of research needed include empirical quantitative studies done in controlled experimental conditions, action research involving classroom teachers whose experience lends a degree of validity unavailable elsewhere, and qualitative studies that portray rich, textured ethnographic descriptions of life in classrooms where interdisciplinary teaching and learning are practiced.

CONCLUSION

The idea of approaching the school curriculum from an interdisciplinary perspective rather than on the basis of separate subjects is a compelling idea. We know that separating academic disciplines for scholarly purposes probably makes sense, but even that premise can be questioned in light of the crossing of frontiers of, for example, biology and psychology, or genetics and linguistics. But for children and adolescents, who are still in the process of adapting, organizing, and otherwise constructing their own schema, such an artificial separation probably makes little sense. On the other hand, students can readily understand the purpose of a project or an activity based on an interesting theme or issue. (See Figure 1.1.)

We also know that schools are often a curious place where large numbers of people, students and teachers, congregate but are expected to work separately and only rarely to collaborate. Obviously interdisciplinary studies is a way of bringing people together. Teachers who have become involved in interdisciplinary teaching have told us that they are really getting to know their colleagues for the first time even though they may have worked next door to them for years. Students, too, because of the project nature of interdisciplinary studies, are given greater opportunity to work with each other. Such experiences surely work to the greater benefit of teachers and students.

On the other hand, we feel that the claims made in the name of interdisciplinary curriculum are at times extravagant, and will only raise hopes beyond reasonable expectation. As you approach the curriculum from an interdisciplinary perspective, we recommend that you do so for reasons of collegiality and real world application. But if you are expecting that such a move will result in higher test scores, we can only say that raising test scores is a complex proposition that involves the home and community as well as the school.

And perhaps this is the time and place to say that higher test scores, a very admirable goal, are not alone a sufficient reason for having schools. Both authors have spent a considerable amount of time in Russian schools. There is little doubt that the test scores of Russian students are superior to those of American students. But consider the system that they have lived in as a way of life. Higher test scores alone have not improved the quality of life in Russia nor in the other former Communist countries of Eastern Europe. School is also about social intelligence, citizenship, participation, and decision making. We are not mak-

FIGURE 1.1 ARGUMENTS FOR AND AGAINST INTEGRATING THE CURRICULUM

Arguments for integrating the curriculum

- Psychological / Developmental - Research in developmental and cognitive psychology suggests individuals learn best when encountering ideas connected to one another.
- Sociocultural - The current curriculum, especially in the secondary school, is fundamentally obsolete and does not address the needs, interests, and capacities of today's students.
- Motivational - The integrated curriculum de-emphasizes rote learning and content coverage, and because it is often organized around student-selected themes and provides for choice, it will enhance student interest and motivation.
- Pedagogical - The traditional curriculum is so vast and intractable that educators cannot hope to cover all the so-called essentials for productive living, and therefore they should focus their efforts on providing experiences leading toward internalization of positive attitudes toward learning.

Obstacles to successful curriculum integration

- The trivialization problem - It is sometimes appropriate for teachers to address ideas within a single content area, and that some ideas are best understood without introducing confusing or inconsequential subject matter.

FIGURE 1.1 ARGUMENTS FOR AND AGAINST INTEGRATING THE CURRICULUM, CONTINUED

- The "skills" problem - A number of educators maintain that students can attempt interdisciplinary work only after they have mastered some elements of disciplinary knowledge, and if integration activities dominate the curriculum, there will be inadequate time to teach these skills.
- The teacher knowledge problem - If teachers lack knowledge and skills within multiple disciplines, their ability to integrate those disciplines is highly problematic.
- The school structure problem - Many teachers have never experienced subject integration themselves, being products of discipline based schooling throughout their lives, meaning vast retraining and reconceptualizing must take place.
- The assessment problem - The mode of assessment in most school systems is not able to effectively assess students' attainment of deep understanding, the stated goal of integrated learning.

****

Source: Adapted from Mason, T.C. (1996). Integrated Curricula: Potential and Problems. *Journal of Teacher Education, 47*(4), 263–270.

ing an argument for ignoring test scores. To do so would be folly. So the best answer is to raise test scores and to meet participatory needs as well. This is the spirit in which we urge you to consider interdisciplinary studies. Professional judgment, whether in education or in some other field, is a difficult, complex enterprise.

REFERENCES

Altshuler, K. (1991). The interdisciplinary classroom. *The Physics Teacher, 29* (7), pp. 428–429.

Anderson, K. (1991). Interdisciplinary inquiry. *School Arts, 91*, (3), p. 4.

Aschbacher, P.R. (1991). Humanitas: A thematic curriculum. *Educational Leadership, 49*(2), pp. 16–19.

Aschbacher, P.R., & Herman, J.L. (1989). The Humanitas program evaluation final report, 1988–89. Los Angeles: UCLA Center for the Study of Evaluation.

Brophy, J., & Alleman, J. (1991). A caveat: curriculum integration isn't always a good idea. *Educational Researcher, 49*(2), p. 66.

Busshman, J.H. (1991). Reshaping the secondary curriculum. *The Clearing House, 65*(2), pp. 83–85.

Cotton, K. (1995). *Effective schooling practices: A research synthesis 1995 update*. Portland, OR: Northwest Regional Educational Laboratory.

Dewey, J. (1913). *Interest and Effort in Education*. Boston: Houghton Mifflin.

Everett, M. (1992). Developmental interdisciplinary schools for the twenty-first century. *The Education Digest, 57*(7), pp. 57–59.

Jacobs, H.H. (Ed). (1989). *Interdisciplinary curriculum: design and implementation*. Alexandria, VA: ASCD.

Joyce, B. & Weil,. (1996). *Models of teaching*. Needham Heights, MA: Allyn & Bacon.

Lake, K. (1994). *School improvement research series VIII: Integrated curriculum*. Portland, OR: Northwest Regional Educational Laboratory.

Lee, V.E., & Smith, J.B. (1994a). *Effects of high school restructuring and size gains in achievement and engagement for early secondary school students.* Madison, WI: Center on Organization and Restructuring of Schools.

Lee, V.E., & Smith, J.B. (1994b). High school restructuring and student achievement. *Issues in Restructuring Schools: Issue Report No. 7.* Madison, WI: Center on Organization and Restructuring of Schools.

Mason, T.C. (1996). Integrated curricula: potential and problems. *Journal of Teacher Education, 47*(4), pp. 263–270.

Morrow, L.M., Pressley, M., & Smith, J.K. (1995). *The effect of a literature-based program integrated into literacy and science instruction on achievement, use, and attitudes toward literacy and science.* Reading Research Report no. 37. Athens, GA: National Reading Research Center.

Post, T.R., Ellis, A.K., Humphreys, A.H., & Buggey, L.J. (1997). *Interdisciplinary curriculum: themes for teaching.* Upper Saddle River, N.J.: Merrill / Prentice-Hall.

Sowell, T. (1995). *The Vision of the Annointed.* New York: Basic Books.

Spady, W.G., & Marshall, K.J. (1991). Beyond traditional outcome-based education. *Educational Leadership,49*(2), pp. 67–72.

Vars, G. (1991). Integrated curriculum in historical perspective. *Educational Leadership, 49*(2), pp. 14–15.

Vygotsky, L.S. (1962). *Thought and Language.* Cambridge, MA: MIT Press.

Walker, D. (1990). *Fundamentals of Curriculum.* Orlando, FL: Harcourt Brace Jovanovich.

2

From Teaching to Learning

The Discovery Experience

There are two senses of the word "discovery." The first sense of discovery is that of "big D" discovery. The second is that of "little d" discovery. Big D discoveries are world-class, original discoveries, the kind that make their way into the history books and the biographies and which become the stuff of epic proportion. Little d discoveries are the kind that you and I make along the way with little or no claim to originality but which are new to us and often immensely satisfying. The fact that someone else may have previously made the same or similar discovery does not take away from the pleasure we feel when we have found out something for ourselves.

In the curriculum experience at its best, there is a happy convergence of Big D and little d discoveries. A curriculum that is focused on the Big D discoveries of Marie Curie, James Cook, Lewis and Clark, or Marco Polo, for example, leaves plenty of room for students and teachers to make their own little d discoveries. The spirit is the same. The quest is not qualitatively different. The theme of integration emerges. Text is merged with experience. Students and teachers become members of the expedition: they are there with Marco Polo on the Old Silk Road, Captain Cook at Botany Bay, and Lewis and Clark at Fort Clatsop.

But there is more to the discovery metaphor than vicarious experience, valuable as that may be in enriching our lives. There is the sense of discovery that occurs when a gifted teacher insists against the odds that students should have leather, hidebound journals just as Lewis and Clark did. And the quest begins. There is the discovery that happens when a student sits down on the floor with a map spread out before her and her fingers begin ever so slowly to traverse the ancient caravan routes across Central Asia, and she realizes for the first time in her life that a map is a tool of wonder. There is the discovery that emerges when a student collects botanic specimens and preserves and classifies them in much the same way that adventurers before him did.

And best of all there are the discoveries that occur along the way in shared experience. Students discover that working together on projects too big for one person opens up undreamed of possibilities. This is the stuff of pageants, fairs, and fieldtrips. One of the abiding tragedies of our time is the growing privatism of human experience. The willingness to sequester ourselves alone at home in front of a television, computer, or video screen draws us into a vortex of increasing isolation from the give-and-take of shared existence.

Students and teachers who work together on shared adventures of discovery experience something that does not happen when people work alone. They experience the transcendent moments that cannot be achieved in isolation. It is the feeling of camraderie and *esprit de corps*, of belonging to something, that happens to members of athletic teams, the participants in a play, clubs, scout groups, church groups, and other social groups. Group experience that achieves true integration meets a profound human need for affiliation, belonging, and friendship.

CURRICULUM AS A DISCIPLINARY CONSTRUCT

An interdisciplinary curriculum is an integrated curriculum, and to understand the implications of such an idea we must explore the curriculum and its potential to serve teachers and students. First of all there is the idea of curriculum as a disciplinary construct. This means that scholarly disciplines serve as the basis of the course of study. There is nothing particularly new or insightful about this observation. It is merely a way of acknowledging that such disciplines as the natural sciences, English, mathematics, history, art, etc., are the building blocks of what is to be learned at school.

If one accepts as reasonable the assumption that the scholarly disciplines are a place to start, and they are, then the question of how to configure them into something meaningful for teachers and students follows. The time-honored approach actually comes from the universities. There, at levels of advanced scholarship, disciplines are treated as distinct entities for purposes of in-depth examination and development by professors and students. Specialization and separation dominate. This practice is sometimes of questionable value even at this level, but it has, by and large, served the purpose of producing scholars and advancing the frontiers of knowledge.

In 1892, when the then-fledgling National Education Association (NEA) commissioned the Committee of Ten, chaired by Harvard University President Charles Eliot, to produce a coherent secondary school curriculum, the Committee took its cues from the university curriculum of the time. This was a curriculum composed of separate subjects taught to students by expert teachers. The teacher's expertise was established on the basis of a knowledge of subject matter and not so much in teaching ability . In essence, the Committee took the university curriculum and presented it to the secondary school. Whether or not this was a wise thing to do has been debated for more than a century. But the Committee's influence was powerful, and we continue to follow many of its recommendations today.

The disciplinary approach to curriculum at the school level rests on several interesting assumptions, not all of which may be valid. The idea is to assign teachers who are more or less experts in a single subject to instruct students daily in a given discipline. Students are expected to attend to that discipline for an appointed time, generally about an hour, before they move on to their next class which repeats the pattern with different content. This happens about five times per day. The whole notion is that students guided by a knowledgeable teacher can concentrate their attention on, say, earth science, in some degree of depth, thereby themselves becoming, if not experts, at least reasonably well acquainted with the subject at hand. In the next class, they concentrate their attention on mathematics, and so on.

Over time a student who takes enough of these courses and who learns from them is said to have a general education, more, in fact, devoted to breadth of coverage than to depth. Of course, there are some subjects in the curriculum that are not disciplinary, for example, home economics or word processing. They are considered to be practical arts or life skills courses and are quite valuable, but the core of the curriculum is comprised of the various separately taught and separately learned disciplines. The reason the student is said to have a general education is twofold: on the one hand, he or she has taken a wide range of classes, and on the other hand the student is expected to be able to link the learning from the various classes into a coherent whole, or to be able to achieve what might be called a sense of integrity about his or her learning. This is a noble assumption, one that is basic to the foundation of a democratic society which can work well only with an educated citizenry.

SINGLE DISCIPLINARY APPROACH

We know that it is common to teach subjects separately, and we know the rationale: a knowledgeable teacher offers an in-depth focus for students. What we are less sure of indeed is how successful this approach is for senior high school students, much less for middle school students. The question must be asked whether the curriculum is best delivered this way or perhaps in some alternate form. The truth of the matter is that conclusive proof of the superiority of one means of curriculum structure over another is lacking, and as often as not we are left with competing points of view rather than final arguments.

The single disciplinary approach can be likened to a daily reading of the comics in a newspaper. Each comic strip or cartoon is self-contained, having nothing to do with the others. The reader merely superficially considers one before moving on to the next one. Except for a pompous few devoted to political satire, there is no pretense of serious teaching by the writer/illustrator or of serious learning by the reader, whose only goal is to be temporarily amused. No connections are even expected to occur between or among the various comics, and no common themes appear except as they might coincidentally touch on topics of interest in the society at large. For the comics, this is fine, but what about the school curriculum?

For starters, the school curriculum is serious business, and the purpose of the comics is entertainment. Beyond that, however, three arguments for changing the structure and nature of the school curriculum for middle school students can be advanced. The first of these arguments has to do with the strange historical phenomenon that has resulted in the combination of a university-type subject matter delivery system (right down to the 50 minute periods) with a program of custody or daycare. Let us take a moment to examine this issue.

The reason that university courses are 50 minutes to one hour in length is that this is about how long it takes to deliver a well thought-out lecture followed by a few questions from an audience. The idea is that students might attend from one to three lectures on any given day, generally with time in between classes. It is not unusual for students to find that on some days they do not even have classes. And when they do have classes, the number of hours spent in attendance is limited. What the students do between classes is up to them. They might study or do some research in the library; they might take a nap; they might meet friends for coffee. Regardless of what they do, there is time built in for them to reflect on what they have learned in class or to recover from the concentration of listening, taking notes, or discussing issues. The university curriculum is simply not configured in such a way as to force students to take one class after another each day for six hours. To expect such a thing would be to ignore the most fundamental principles of learning. It would create a whirlwind pace rather than the more leisurely pace required of serious learning.

Now the curious thing about all of this is that university students are more mature learners than middle school students, and they represent a more select, academically talented clientele than one finds in the typical middle school. Why, therefore, do we ask less of university students than of adolescents in terms of number of class hours per week? And why do we give university students more time to reflect on their learning than we give to younger people who reason would dictate, require more time to reflect on what they have been taught?

Of course, the reason why we have traditionally kept younger students busy moving from one class to the next has nothing to do with learning or with time for reflective thought. It is a daycare or custodial arrangement. Thus the 50 minute period is primarily an artifact of university-level instruction placed into a situation where there is little or nothing in the way of a rationale to support it other than tradition. Granted, our students need some form of responsible daycare. We simply cannot turn them loose the way university students are between classes. But think about the mind-numbing process of sending ordinary achievers from class to class each hour in a way that higher achieving, older university students are not asked to do. At some point, the benefits of instruction are overwhelmed by overload and disconnected superficiality in such a way that no serious person would acknowledge it as being intellectually stimulating.

Thus we have a situation where younger, unselected students are asked, in the name of learning, to take more classes per day than mature, academically selected students. That is, they are expected to absorb more lectures and presentations than their older, more advanced counterparts. Those who doubt that students at the middle school level and above are spending their class time listening to lectures should check the research data which show that the single most probable classroom event at the secondary school level is teacher talk. And as though that were not enough, we allow no open time between classes where students might reflect, study, rest, or gather socially.

And lastly, we offer students separate courses expecting them to do what their teachers do not apparently do, that is, tie the knowledge, skills, and values of the various courses together into some kind of coherent whole. Theoretically, at least, the idea of general education is that the various components assume a measure of wholeness. Perhaps a few students see the relationships among and between separate subjects, but most surely do not. If this were really an important goal, then teachers ought to plan together and to offer courses that have obvious links with one another. This could be accomplished through synchronized assignments, cross-disciplinary projects, and other similar means.

INTERDISCIPLINARY CURRICULUM

One reasonable answer to the deep-seated problem of a "fractionalized" curriculum, one composed of separately delivered and unrelated pieces and which is disconnected from life, is the interdisciplinary approach to teaching and learning. There is nothing new about an interdisciplinary curriculum. It has been around in one form or another for a long time. Unfortunately, it has not always delivered on its promise. Let's examine why this might be and what can be done to remedy the situation.

We begin with a modest assumption: separately taught disciplines can be connected in such a way that they offer strategic support to one another while maintaining their own integrity and sense of proportion. This is a modest assumption but one that is often ignored or violated in the rush to combine subjects. To address this assumption we must pose a fundamental question. How can the various subjects that traditionally contribute individually to the curriculum instead contribute collectively?

The most common answer to our question is to begin by selecting themes or topics that have great academic and socially energizing potential. The themes must be powerful, capable of drawing on all the typically disparate elements of the school curriculum. The themes must be educationally worthwhile because they are, after all, assuming priority over something that we have agreed is important, that is, the school curriculum as it is traditionally configured. The traditional curriculum is not something to be surrendered lightly. Whatever we do to change the content itself, and the organizational pattern and/or delivery system had better be an improvement or we shouldn't attempt it.

Assuming the possibility of identifying worthwhile themes, the next task is to figure out how to bring the key elements of each separate discipline, its knowledge, skills, and values, into play in such a way that the theme is not merely interesting to students and teachers but educationally purposeful as well. We must be convinced that the mathematics, literature, art, science, history, etc., that emerge are faithfully represented. This is not easy to do. This is no time to retreat to superficial treatments, to the slighting of certain subjects, or to the selection or frivolous content and themes.

The Journeys of Discovery interdisciplinary curriculum for students in grades four through eight is based on themes that have a rich potential for depth of content and which demand the best of each contributory discipline. The discovery theme has sustaining curricular value, and its variations are virtually unlimited. Thus major texts and subtexts emerge. While the theme is played out principally around the recorded journeys of such luminaries as Herodotus of the Ancient World, Marco Polo of the Medieval World, James Cook of the world of the Enlightenment, and Lewis and Clark of the New World, a number of related journeys complement the major curricular themes.

The idea that curriculum could be organized around the theme of discovery and discoverers is meant to be exemplary of the content/conceptual potential of interdisciplinary approaches in general as much as anything else. Other potentially engaging themes could as well include "invention and inventors," "creativity and creators," "leadership and leaders," "revolutions and revolutionaries," "the arts and artists," etc. The main thing is to choose a theme that can draw upon all curricular areas with authenticity and which has the capability to join the separate disciplines as contributors to large projects and thoughtful activities.

INTEGRATION OF SUBJECT MATTER

One of the goals of an interdisciplinary curriculum is to bring students and teachers closer to the frontiers of knowledge through access to original source materials, principally in the form of diaries, journals, logs, and other forms of first person accounts. Taken on these terms, the curriculum has the potential to turn students into historians, geographers, mathematicians, scientists, and artists. Far too often students and teachers work with processed textbook accounts of the great reach of the human spirit, denying themselves the pleasure and excitement of taking original source material and trying to make sense of it for themselves. This is where the encounter with true spirit of education begins, with one's thoughts about something worthwhile.

But this is only the beginning. The teacher's task is to figure out the possibilities of such original source material to connect with the skills and knowledge students will need in an uncertain future. This is the role of problem-solving, the mysterious business of preparation, incubation, illumination, and verification. But teachers have to make sure that something else happens beyond the choice of worthwhile content studied in a problem-solving mode. They have to ensure that integration occurs not merely with curriculum content, but with the people who study the curriculum as well.

INTEGRATION OF TEACHERS

The first line of integration must occur within the teaching staff. It simply will not do for teachers to withdraw into their respective shells of subject matter expertise while making the disclaimer that they don't know much, if anything, about other areas of the curriculum. In the interdisciplinary approach, each teacher must see him/herself as an integral part of a strategic whole. Each teacher must bring a special expertise or interest to the table, but each teacher must also engage the other areas of the curriculum thoughtfully. This begins to happen when teachers talk and plan with each other about an important cross-cutting theme, one that truly demands the insights of each teacher and his/her specialty. Thus teachers must experience integration if they want to integrate the subject they teach. An important rule of thumb to keep in mind about integration is "first people, then subjects."

INTEGRATION OF STUDENTS AND COMMUNITY

Once the teaching staff begins to feel integrated, and they have chosen a worthwhile theme that calls on the various disciplines, the next step is to commit to integrating students. At its best, interdisciplinary teaching and learning is project -oriented. The best projects, like the best journeys of discovery, take teamwork. Somehow the feeling that we really need each other in order to carry out the visionary projects that will be undertaken this year needs to be communicated to students. Interdisciplinary curriculum must call on all the disciplines in order to be successful, but even more than that, it must call upon all students to share with each other their gifts, talents, energy, good will, and hard work.

Now, having integrated subject matter, faculty, and students, what else is left? This is no time to stop. The logical place to go from here is to integrate parents and other interested community members into the curriculum. It can be done, and it must be done in order to achieve the highest levels of success. One of the surest ways to raise achievement in a school is to involve interested adults in some meaningful ways. Where parents feel informed and involved, a whole host of problems are diminished.

The school that can bring students, teachers, families, and community members together around the abiding ideas of a thoughtful curriculum anchored in purposeful knowledge, skills, and values is one that will prosper not only academically but will find support in other areas when it needs it.

THE TEACHING/LEARNING PROCESS

In the discovery experience, students must take the initiative for their learning. The teacher's role shifts from teller and director to organizer and guide. To cite a specific example, in the *Journeys of Discovery* curriculum this change in emphasis is significant. The teacher assumes much the same role that Lewis and Clark assumed in their epic journey, or that any other good leaders assume. Their role, and likewise that of a discovery-oriented teacher, is to ensure that the trip is well-organized, that preparation, support, and follow-through are in place as much as possible as students and teachers together venture across an uncharted landscape of learning. It is also incumbent upon teachers in this context to show the way just as a good guide leads the way. The metaphor of teacher as guide allows for leadership under a lead explorer whose experience, know-how, and insight facilitate the processes of inquiry, invention, documentation, and creativity. Good leadership is a balancing act that provides structure without being overbearing, that points the way while recognizing that more than one path may get someone from here to there. These are fundamental changes in teacher role, and they are not easy changes for some teachers to make. The changes are often difficult for students to make as well, particularly those students whose success has been based in large measure on their skill at doing what they are told to do, a common trait of many "high achievers." The problem for other-directed students is that it is difficult for them to learn on their own. They may be good at responding to direction and to completing assignments given to them by teachers, but this represents an impoverished sense of what it means to learn. The discoverer, on the other hand, need not wait around to be told what to do. He/she knows how to move ahead by posing questions, constructing hypotheses, gathering data, trying to make sense of things, and by reaching conclusions. So the fundamental, underlying goal structure changes from other-directed to self-directed. For both teachers and students, the goal becomes an enabling goal: to set oneself free to become a self-sustaining learner whose desire to learn carries on beyond the school experience into lifelong learning.

ESSENCE OF DISCOVERY

Many scholars have attempted to capture the essence of the discovery experience, but probably no one has equaled the insight of Graham Wallas when it comes to reducing the process to a few well-chosen words. Wallas conceived of the discovery process as something that happens in four identifiable stages. The stages are not necessarily linear in function, and there is no doubt a considerable amount of slipping back and forth from stage to stage as one discovers something. He called the stages *preparation, incubation, illumination,* and *verification*. The words are so descriptive as to nearly speak for themselves. Still, let's spend a little time with each.

Preparation. The first stage in the discovery process is preparation. This stage is so often underestimated and overlooked by the less-than-serious that most attempts at discovery learning lead to frustration and abandonment, resulting in the "we tried that" syndrome so familiar to teachers. Preparation represents a kind of blend of attitude and information. The old adage that chance favors the prepared mind is useful to remember in this context. An attitude of openness, especially to the seemingly outlandish and impossible is necessary, but it must be supported by a desire to know one's object of study.

The somewhat apocryphal story of Isaac Newton's discovery of the so-called law of gravity while sitting under an apple tree is a good example of attitude and information coming together. When the apple fell to earth from the tree, Newton employed his deep knowledge of the attraction of one mass to another, the greater mass pulling the lesser mass toward its center. But people had long been aware of this. The key was Newton's openness to the cause as well as the easily observable result. Thus it was that Newton realized before others that the attraction of one object to another actually represents a *universal* principle that works in any setting anywhere. Earlier work had been done by other scientists, including Galileo and Kepler. Thus Newton's knowledge was more than just his own scholarly judgment and intuition. He was able to take the existent knowledge and refine it into a mathematical formula that illustrates that every particle of matter in the universe attracts every other particle with a force that is directly proportional to the product of their masses and inversely proportional to the square of the distance between them. He expressed the formula mathematically as:

$$F = \frac{Gm \times m}{d}$$

where F is the force of attraction, m and m are the masses of the two objects, d is the distance between the two objects, and G is a universal gravitational constant. The point is to underscore that Newton depended heavily upon knowledge he had gained from a variety of sources as a way of preparing for this discovery, and he still would not have made it had he not been open to the possibilities. Knowledge is essential to discovery, but not inert knowledge learned merely as an exercise or to pass an exam; knowledge that is organic, that is to say alive, is the kind of knowledge that sustains the learner with a spirit of openness to new ideas. We'll return to this example later as we examine subsequent stages of the Graham Wallas discovery model.

To return to the *Journeys of Discovery* curriculum, the discovery metaphor is brought to concrete example in the epic trek of Lewis and Clark. Theirs was to be a discovery process that unfolded over several years during which time they ranged out to the Pacific and back. These were resourceful people to be sure, but the *preparations* they took for the journey were in large measure the reason for its ultimate success. The same thing could be said for the journeys of other successful explorers.

This is not the place to furnish all the details of preparation that went into Lewis and Clark's journey of discovery, but this brief and typical passage of instruction from President Thomas Jefferson to Captain Meriwether Lewis illustrates how seriously this stage of discovery was taken:

> Your observations are to be taken with great pains & accuracy, to be entered distinctly & intelligibly for others as well as yourself, to comprehend all the elements necessary, with the aid of the usual tables, to fix the latitude and longitude of the places at which they were taken & are to be rendered to the war office, for the purpose of having the calculations made concurrently by the proper persons with the U.S . . . .

The fact is that Lewis and Clark ventured nowhere where some people had not been before them, but the difference between their true journey of discovery and the wanderings of others illustrates the power of preparation. A final point about preparation in the discovery process is in order. Discovery by its very nature takes one into the unknown, and the unknown is always fraught with peril. Whether we consider a young learner attempting to discover on his/her own without being told all the answers or whether we consider the triumphs and disasters that have befallen both the American and Russian space programs, even careful preparation is no guarantee of a secure voyage. But the very lack of a guarantee is the key to the excitement of the discovery approach to learning.

Incubation. The mysterious process known as *incubation* represents Wallas' second stage of discovery. This stage has been the undoing of more than one would-be discoverer, whether teacher or student. Good preparation has a sense of activity about it as one organizes the adventure. Incubation, on the other hand, is a kind of waiting game, as the image of a hen sitting on a nest of eggs would suggest. Actually though, much is happening during this seemingly passive stage. This is a time to ponder and consider a problem, to allow oneself the luxury of thinking ahead in time while reflecting back on what has happened so far. In some respect this is an unpredictable, nonlinear process that can give the appearance of time wasted.

Incubation is necessary because it slows one down from the temptation to move ahead too quickly following the preparation stage. This is a time to be deliberate, patient, and thoughtful. It can also be a time of reflection and even second-guessing of one's original premise. To attempt to rush this stage is to force the process. It makes no more sense than to try to speed up the blossoming of a flower or the hatching of an egg. In concrete form, a teacher and class that have been writing journals of their own discoveries as they study the explorations of Lewis and Clark need to spend time reflecting on the meaning of what they are doing.

In some sense, the idea of incubation is akin to metacognition, or thinking about the activities, processes, etc., in which one becomes so busily engaged. It is useful to remember that one definition of a fanatic is a person who redoubles his efforts, having lost sight of the original goal. It is not unusual to see teachers who are thoroughly committed to working harder without reflecting on what it means to work well. Perhaps the so-called "add-on" curriculum from which we all suffer is a product of our failure to reflectively consider what it is we are trying to accomplish.

A few years ago a book was published, that sold in the multiple thousands, titled *Teach More, Faster*. The thesis of this book for teachers was that they could cover more information and skills if only they were more efficient. The book showed them how to become more efficient. Perhaps some application of the incubation process would have led teachers to consider whether teaching and learning are really about efficiency.

Illumination. The stage called *illumination* by Wallas is perhaps the best known aspect of discovery. This is where the proverbial light bulb comes on, the kind cartoonists like to show lighting up above the thinker's head. This is where the discovery takes place. It is the time of insight, of new perspectives, of things becoming clear that were unclear. What was unclear or shrouded in mystery is now perceived or has at least become less mysterious.

Maybe the best known case of illumination in recorded history is the legendary story of Archimedes, who ran naked through the streets of Athens shouting "Eureka!" ("I have found it!") when he realized that an object will displace its density when placed in water. Apparently, Archimedes had been "incubating" in the bathtub trying to solve the problem of determining whether a crown made for the king was in fact solid gold. The answer came to him in a flash when he realized that all objects displace their density in water, and gold has a certain density that is different from other metals.

Thomas Edison used to practice the incubation stage during those famous catnaps he would take at his laboratory in Menlo Park, New Jersey. Edison, who typically slept only a few hours each night, would sit down from time to time in an easy chair for a short rest. He would hold a steel ball bearing in each hand, and as he relaxed and dozed off the ball bearings drop onto metal pie plates placed strategically on the floor below. The sound would wake him, and he would immediately write down his thoughts of the moment. Edison felt that many of his most productive ideas came during these times. This procedure has been validated by recent brain research which informs us that our brain often secretes creativity-rich alpha waves as we begin to sleep.

Verification. The final phase of the discovery experience, *verification,* involves carrying out and testing the plan to see if it works. It is the time of putting ideas to the test to see if they are practical. This is a time of completion, of validation, and of checking up. Middle school students who were involved in an archeological dig wanted to know whether the procedures they were using were authentic. How could they verify this? An anthropologist at a nearby university helped them with the necessary procedures of carefully cleaning the objects, tagging them, and classifying them according to form and function.

To verify means to ascertain the truth or accuracy of something. Thus, verification implies also a search for meaning and satisfaction. Students and teachers who wish to verify a learning experience will reflect on what happened. Such reflection often takes the form of discussions in which all participants are given the opportunity the express their thoughts and feelings. Verification represents a quest to determine to what extent the experience was meaningful, and why. It is a time to consider whether things could have been done differently, and to try to determine not merely if something worked, but how well it worked. It is a time for journal entries written in a reflective mode and a time of assessment. Because the discovery experience is ongoing, verification happens along the way as well as at the end of a discovery. What students and teachers themselves discover is that one discovery leads to another, and that knowledge is connected in that respect. Thus, the verification that happens along the way during a unit of study is what we call *formative verification* while the verification that happens when it is time to look back on an experience at its conclusion is called *summative verification*. Formative verification keeps discoverers on track, while summative verification assesses the whole from the vantage point of hindsight.

INQUIRY AND THE JOURNEYS OF DISCOVERY

A comment often made by middle school teachers goes something like this: "I'd love to do inquiry teaching, but I'm not sure that I even know what it is." Also, one hears such comments as: "I guess I've been doing inquiry for years; we just never called it that."

Part of the problem is the absence of a publicly agreed-upon definition of "inquiry." Of course, inquiry is done in science, social science, the humanities, mathematics, the arts, and other subjects, and in each case the emphasis is somewhat different. Let us offer a definition that should be a useful place to start. *Inquiry is a process in which we pose questions about some phenomenon and attempt to discover meaning by making inferences about the answers we obtain.* So, to do inquiry one typically begins by posing an empirical question, that is, one that can be answered through the gathering and evaluating of data. An example of this might be, "What was childhood like for our grandparents?" Once we have our question (in this case a historical question) we can begin to think about gathering the information (data) necessary to give us answers. The techniques of data gathering—whether a survey, a reading of old diaries, interviews with grandparents, or an investigation of secondary sources such as magazines or newspapers from past years—all could all be considered forms of inquiry if they help to answer our question.

The questions we pose are what *guide* our inquiry. The answers we obtain are what *inform* our discovery. This is the relationship between inquiry and discovery. One inquires in order to discover. Inquiry questions are questions that can be answered by gathering information and putting the information together in new ways.

This may sound rather simple, but take a moment to contrast inquiry questions with, say, philosophical questions. A philosophical question cannot be answered primarily by gathering information. If we were to ask, "What is the most beautiful color?" we may find opinions ranging from blue, red, green, etc., but no amount of information, not even a majority opinion, will yield a definitive answer to the question, which is one of personal preference. A related inquiry question for a school attempting to choose school colors might be, "What is the most popular color among primary students in our school?" A survey of preferences would allow us to discover the range of opinion or choice on the matter.

More often inquiry and discovery are contrasted with the kind of traditional learning that goes on at school. This type of learning, based on what is called didactic teaching, involves teaching students a skill, such as a particular mathematics operation, and then having them follow up by practicing the operation in the form of problems or exercises. Didactic teaching in history might typically involve having students read a passage from a textbook or listen to a lecture followed either by a discussion or some form of written assignment. There is, of course, nothing wrong with didactic teaching when it is done in moderation. In fact, it is a useful way to teach certain skills and knowledge. The biggest learning problems associated with didactic teaching are: (1)its over-use and (2)its failure to involve students actively. When it becomes a day-in, day-out routine, it loses its potential to reach students in meaningful ways. This is often the beginning of such commonly held student attitudes as, "Social studies was always boring for me because it was just a bunch of names, dates, and places." Or, "I never could see the point of all the math problems we had to work on because I'm not going to use that stuff anyway." These, of course, are perceptions of reality. The same experience might have affected someone else differently, but the truth is that in far too many cases the perception of school life as boring, irrelevant, etc., is closely associated with an overabundance of didacticism.

Inquiry and discovery are active learning experiences that involve question posing, data gathering, analysis, and, always, a search for meaning. We ask a question. We gather information. And we try to make sense of our information by turning it into knowledge. We can ask questions about the past (historical inquiry). We can ask questions about the present (descriptive inquiry). Or we can establish special conditions in order to study something (experimental inquiry).

Inquiry and discovery invariably involve problem solving. These terms are closely linked. If we decided to answer the question, "What is a typical school day for Japanese students?" we would try to *describe* life in a Japanese school. Therefore, this would be *descriptive* research. If we asked the question, "What was a typical school day for children in Colonial New England?" we have posed a *historical* question. If we asked the question, "How will our classroom be different if we change the seating arrangement into a circle?" then we have posed an *experimental* question. If we asked the question, "What extracurricular programs would the students in our school like the most?" we have posed a *survey* question. Notice that all these questions can be "answered" by gathering information and, more importantly, by discovering meaning in the information.

Inquiry and discovery as teaching/learning modes are fundamental to interdisciplinary curriculum efforts. This is why students must have access to original source material, including such rich sources of information as the diaries of Lewis and Clark, the ship's logs of Captain James Cook, the writings of the historian Herodotus, and the accounts of the travels of Marco Polo.

SHIFT IN EMPHASIS

The whole idea of the inquiry/discovery paradigm is to shift the center of gravity in what it means to be a student. Students are accustomed to working with what are known as "tertiary" materials. Tertiary sources are those that have been processed by others, most commonly into the form of textbooks, workbooks, etc. Such sources are not the kind where one searches for meaning on the basis of one's own investigations. Rather, meaning (at least the kind of meaning the author wishes the reader to find) is presented to the student. This may seem efficient at first glance. Why, after all, waste time allowing adolescents to search for meaning in old diaries, on archaeological digs, or doing complicated projects when it can be given to them in the form of lecture, text reading, or problems? While such a question may seem loaded with irony, consider the evidence of how students are typically taught. Without getting into too much detail here, we can assure the reader that the research evidence is overwhelming that most of the teaching most of the time in American schools is didactic.

When the shift in the center of gravity of what it means to be a student occurs, three things follow. First, students must take on the responsibility of finding their own answers to difficult questions. Former Secretary of Education John Gardner once noted that a fundamental problem of school life is that teachers give students cut flowers when they should be giving them seeds. What he meant by this is that too often students are unwittingly deprived of both the joy and the responsibility of discovering meaning in learning. This happens when they are denied the raw materials of learning, that is, original sources and the investigative experiences that follow from their use.

Secondly, motivation to learn shifts from being the teacher's responsibility to that of the students. Perhaps you have noticed that it is typical of lesson plans that they have a step in which the teacher is supposed to motivate the class. Why is this so? The answer is that somehow the teaching profession has been sold the idea that what is to be learned in school needs to be made attractive in order to gain students' genuine attention. This is generally true. But the fallacy in reasoning is to look to the teacher rather than to the material itself as the answer. No doubt teaching is an art form that calls on complex abilities. But the more we allow the center of gravity to shift to the teacher away from the student, the more dependent we make the student, and the more we lessen his/her instincts to find out things without being told.

And thirdly, the conduct of inquiry requires that people work together across disciplinary lines. Most purposeful inquiry/discovery projects are simply too big for one person. They take teamwork. Good school-based inquiry takes inspired teachers who are willing to work together bringing to the table the best of their disciplines. The school experiences that are the most inspiring, that build the most lasting memories are those that involve students working together. When the academic curriculum finally realizes what the athletic curriculum, the drama curriculum, and the other extracurricular areas already know about human needs and learning, then progress will be possible. No wonder Robert Maynard Hutchins observed nearly half a century ago, "Students resort to the extracurriculum because the curriculum is so stupid."

Jean Piaget once noted that telling is not teaching. Teaching is a deeper, more complex art. Piaget thought the teacher's genius is found in his/her ability to organize the environment for learning. Anatole France said it well: "The whole art of teaching is only the art of awakening the natural curiosity of young minds . . . ." The same curiosity, no different in quality at all, is what drove Lewis and Clark to do what they did. It is what summoned young Marco Polo to adventures so far beyond the reach of his wildest dreams as to seem unimaginable even today. And this same curiosity is what drives a teacher to see in a student the possibilities for excellence beyond the student's own wildest hopes and dreams. (See comparisons in Figure 2.1.)

MAKING THE TRANSITION

Here are several practical steps that schools and teachers can take to facilitate the transition from teaching to learning. These steps will work only if teachers are serious about bringing about a fundamental transformation in the ways in which

FIGURE 2.1. COMPARISONS BETWEEN FOCUSES OF TRADITIONAL AND EXPERIENTIAL CURRICULA

TRADITIONAL ORIENTATION	EXPERIENTIAL ORIENTATION
TEACHER	LEARNER
DIRECTION	EXPLORATION
WORKLIKE	PLAYFUL
STANDARDIZED	PERSONALIZED
FORMAL	INFORMAL
TEACHING	LEARNING
LESSONS	EXPERIENCES
DIDACTIC	EXPRESSIVE
SCOPE & SEQUENCE	PROBLEMS/ISSUES
LINEAR	THEMATIC
CENTRALIZED	DECENTRALIZED
UNIFORM	DIFFERENTIATED
TEXTBOOKS	SOURCE MATERIAL
ASSIGNMENTS	CHOICES
ISOLATION	COOPERATION
DISCRETE SUBJECT	CONNECTED LEARNING
SEATWORK/LECTURE	PROJECTS
REPRODUCTION	PRODUCTION
TESTS/GRADES	AUTHENTIC ASSESSMENT

we think about teaching and learning, and indeed the ways in which we think about the purposes of school.

1. MEANINGFULNESS. For too many students, school has very little real meaning. This is true not only for low achievers but for many high achievers as well. Students are given work to do simply because it is part of the curriculum. They are required to complete assignments in order to be able to complete future assignments. Often students are given little or no choice about the work they are expected to do. In the first century A.D., the Roman educator Quintilian introduced the "doctrine of interest." He boldly suggested that not all school work should be contrived ahead of time for students, but that they, students, should be able to study the things that interest them most. He wrote about the individual differences to be found among students, and he suggested that it would be profitable for teachers to study their students in order to find out what they wanted to learn. Centuries later, this thought was echoed by Jean-Jacques Rousseau who suggested that a teacher's first duty was to get to know his students better, because, as he said, "you surely do not know them."

This is the key to meaningful learning: the relationship between teacher and student. A recent study showed that most adolescents say that very few (less than 10 percent) of the teachers they had in school had any meaningful effect on their lives. Those few teachers who did have a meaningful effect on the lives of their students were invariably ones whom the students felt cared personally about the subjects they taught. Thus meaning comes not from carefully prepared lectures or from worksheets prepared by educational experts, but from shared encounters between teacher and student. When teachers take time to listen to their students, wonderful things begin to happen. Meaningful relationships develop, students begin to want to learn on their own. Learning becomes a joy instead of a drudgery.

2. MAKING CONNECTIONS. In a research study directed by one of the authors, ten- and eleven-year old students were given the opportunity to become involved in a class project of their own choosing. The class was asked to decide on some-

thing they would manufacture and sell to other students. For their project they chose to make simple denim-covered folders that other students could use to keep their papers in. They manufactured, advertised, and sold their product. Each day the students worked on the project, dividing the labor among themselves. Many problems arose along the way, and the students had to solve them democratically. Each day, the teacher would spend a few minutes reviewing their work and discussing with them the economic ideas related to what they were doing. She explained such concepts as "supply and demand," "division of labor," and "human and material resources." The students would discuss these ideas as they related to their project.

In a comparison classroom, students studied a textbook on economics. They studied the same concepts that the project students studied. The difference was that the students in the comparison class studied economics as typical abstract school work. At the conclusion of the study, students in both classrooms were tested on their knowledge of economics. The project students achieved much higher scores than did the comparison class. The reasons for the differences in achievement were clear: the project students were able to connect the economic ideas to their personal experience. Thus the ideas had meaning. For the students in the comparison group, it was "in one ear and out the other."

One other thing that emerged from this study is worth noting. The students in the project class worked together, talked together, decided together, etc. As a result, they reported that they made meaningful friendships with one another. A girl who had recently enrolled in the school was assigned to the project class. She had no friends. Life in school was painful and difficult for her. The teachers said that she was a good student but she was very lonely and withdrawn. In the project class she quickly became involved with other students because the students needed to work together. She made several good friends and became a happier person. The students in the comparison classroom were so busy studying their worksheets that they had little or no time for meaningful relationships to develop, either with one another or with the teacher. Therefore, we as teachers desperately need to search for ways to bring about connections between the students' experiences and interests and the academic skills and concepts that we want them to learn.

3. MOTIVATION. Research shows that the motivation to learn a school subject is from 60 to 70 percent the result of prior learning. Thus students who have experienced success in a school subject will be predictably eager to learn more about that subject. Students who have experienced failure will predictably become discouraged. They lose their motivation to learn. They fall behind in their studies and lose their desire to attend school. Their teachers become impatient with them. In time they come to dislike academic learning and anything associated with it. The key to motivation is to realize that almost all students can be successful achievers. Unfortunately, teachers often equate the rate at which a student grasps an idea or skill with learning. But this is wrong thinking on the part of the teacher. It is a proven fact that speed of learning is not the same thing as depth of learning. In fact, some people who learn more slowly are able to learn in greater depth. Some people who learn quickly are not necessarily ultimately better learners than their slower counterparts. Centuries ago, the Greek writer Aesop told the tale of the tortoise and the hare in which he made this very point: the race is not necessarily to the swift; slow but sure wins many races.

When we erroneously equate rate of learning with ability to learn, we leave many students behind who were perfectly capable of learning whatever it was that we were trying to teach. This has disastrous effects because once you fall behind it becomes increasingly difficult to catch up, and your motivation toward further learning is destroyed. Therefore, as teachers you must consider the possibility that perhaps someone is slower to learn because he or she sees the complexities inherent in the material, and is taking a deliberate approach to the subject. But whatever the reason, patience is called for. People who are not patient should not be teachers. Teachers must be the patient sowers of good seed if they wish to reap a bountiful, worthwhile harvest.

4. TEACHING LESS. Jean-Jacques Rousseau wrote that we should teach less, and teach it well. This is a powerful insight. Rather than trying to cover so much material in your teaching,

you should identify the few key ideas that you know are the most important and teach them in depth. Visit them and revisit them using meaningful examples and appropriate applications. If an idea is truly worth learning, it should be complex enough to be examined from a variety of points of view so that it becomes clearer and clearer to those who must learn it.

The great Russian novelist Nikolai Vasilievich Gogol wrote a story called, "The Overcoat," in which a poor bureaucrat saves his money in order to have a tailor make him a handsome winter coat. The coat becomes the most important thing in the man's life. Every day he stops by the tailor's shop to see how his coat is coming along. At night the man dreams of the coat and how fine he will look in it. When the garment is at last finished the man dons it proudly and steps out into the winter night only to be beaten and robbed of his new coat. The story can be read for the writer's style. It can also be read for a glimpse of life in nineteenth century Russia. It is also a study of shattered dreams. But the point is that the story is worth taking one's time over. The parables of Jesus, Aesop, and others have been told for centuries because of the truth they contain. Their modern-day applications are endless. They can be studied over and over because of the insights they provide. Mathematical ideas such as the Pythagorean Theorem and the fixed ratio between the circumference and diameter of a circle ($C= \pi D$) have symmetry and beauty worthy of reflection and application.

Perhaps the best way to teach less and teach it well is as follows:

- Be sure that you can identify the key ideas for whatever you set out to teach.
- Be sure that you do not try to cover too much material at one time.
- Be sure that you allow your students time to talk with one another and reflect on the key ideas of an assignment.
- Be sure that you give your students opportunities to apply the ideas they learn in a variety of ways which emphasize spiritual, practical, aesthetic, and intellectual implications.

5. FROM TEACHING TO LEARNING. It is useful to observe children at play if you wish to make the transition from teaching to learning. They will show how to do it. We are not talking about adult-supervised soccer or baseball for children. That is the opposite of play. (Those are regimented activities which are planned and arbitrated by adults, thereby allowing none of the complexities of mental, moral, and spiritual insight that are possible in true play. Once when one of us attended an adult-supervised game involving ten- and eleven-year old boys and girls an argument broke out over some obscure rule. The children were told to sit down and stay out of the way while the adults quarreled among themselves, thus effectively depriving the children of the opportunity to attempt to resolve a conflict that at the moment had real meaning. These children were not players in the most meaningful sense of the term; they were, rather, game pieces in an adult activity.)

When young children play together in the dirt or in a mud puddle, they spend much of their time discussing ideas and creating imaginary worlds. They invent activities, rules, roles, and so on. To the best of our knowledge, no pedagogue has written up the rules and/or provided worksheets and testing procedures for playing in dirt and mud. Children playing video games also are interesting to watch. It is especially fascinating to listen to their debriefing conversations in which they reflect with each other on the strategies and skills needed to achieve various levels of the game to the point of mastery. Guidebooks are written for the video games, and often a child will devour one searching for ways to master a particular game. But whether we are considering mud puddles or video games, the point is the same, namely, that no one teaches this stuff. You just get involved in the enterprise, do it to the best of your ability, learn from others, and read on your own. These same procedures work in classrooms where the teacher is him/herself excited about learning new things and where he/she has provided an environment filled with interesting things to do and learn about. Learning takes on a playful, informal tone, and a surprising amount gets done. The teacher moves around the room talking to students, mediating their questions, and providing a forum in which group activities and discussions can take place in addition to the individualized work that students carry out.

Students in these environments tend to read more, talk more with their fellow students and teachers, and in general exhibit a greater love of learning than do their counterparts in more traditional classrooms. Why? Because they have made the important transition from being taught to becoming learners.

If we are to make a successful transition into an information age of schooling, teachers must be willing to reconsider their fundamental role. We must be willing to abandon the idea that teaching is telling. We must be willing to embrace the concept of the exploration of ideas by teachers and students working together. We must set aside our thoughts of school based on a production-oriented, industrial model. We must be willing to cross the frontier from teaching to learning.

REFERENCES

Bruner, J. (1996). *The culture of education.* Cambridge, MA: Harvard University Press.

Connelly, F.M., & Ben-Peretz, M. (1997). Teachers, research, and curriculum development. In David Flinders & Stephen Thornton (Eds.). *The curriculum studies reader*, pp.178–187. New York: Routledge.

Dewey, J. (1913). *Interest and effort in education.* Boston: Houghton Mifflin Co.

Drucker, P.F. (1993). *Post-capitalist society.* New York: Harper Collins.

Eisner, E. (1997). Humanistic trends and the curriculum field. In David Flinders & Stephen Thornton (Eds.). *The curriculum studies reader*, pp. 159–166. New York: Routledge.

Ellis, A.K. & Fouts, J. (1994). *Research on school restructuring.* Larchmont, NY: Eye on Education.

Ellis, A.K. & Fouts, J. (1997). *Research on educational innovations: 2nd ed.* Larchmont, NY: Eye on Education.

McCutcheon, G. (1997). Curriculum and the work of teachers. In David Flinders & Stephen Thornton (Eds.). *The curriculum studies reader*, pp.188–197. New York: Routledge.

McLaughlin, M. (1997). Implementation as mutual adaption: Change in classroom organizations. In David Flinders & Stephen Thornton (Eds.). *The curriculum studies reader*, pp. 167–177. New York: Routledge.

Schwab, J. (1997). The practical: A language for curriculum. In David Flinders & Stephen Thornton (Eds.). *The curriculum studies reader*, pp. 101–115. New York: Routledge.

Yelon, S.L. (1996). *Powerful principles of instruction.* White Plains, NY: Longman.

3

Approaches to an Interdisciplinary Curriculum

Teaching an interdisciplinary curriculum can be approached from several different perspectives. The idea behind interdisciplinary studies is that various subjects or disciplines are weaved together in order to more clearly present a concept, idea, principle, or problem. To that end, teachers of an interdisciplinary curriculum look for ways to approach the curriculum that will support the development of cognitive processes and concepts. These approaches rely heavily on several elements that allow them to be used effectively in interdisciplinary studies, including:

- active involvement of students
- a motivating environment that provokes questions and curiosity
- topics of study that are of interest to students

Two approaches that incorporate these elements and seem to work well in teaching and learning an interdisciplinary curriculum are the project approach and a theme-based unit approach.

The Project Approach

The project approach to an interdisciplinary curriculum can be traced to the ideas and work of John Dewey and William Kilpatrick. Leaders in the Progressive era, both Dewey and Kilpatrick suggested that learning should take place through a student-centered curriculum rather than through a teacher-directed curriculum. Dewey specifically called for an inquiry approach to learning, in which students would answer questions and solve problems by following the steps of the scientific method. After identifying a problem or question of interest, students then propose a hypothesis, gather information to answer the question, and finally come to some sort of conclusion. To that end, Dewey proposed an interdisciplinary curriculum centering on theme-oriented projects. Dewey believed that learning should be reflective of "real life" experiences, where the various subjects would be taught and learned in an integrated format, as we find them in our daily activities, problems, and jobs. The project approach reflected these beliefs, and found some success during the Progressive era.

Projects were also championed by William Kilpatrick. Like Dewey, he believed that the child should be at the center of the teaching and learning process, and that "real-life" projects that integrated the various subject areas should be at the heart of the curriculum. In addition, Kilpatrick suggested that students be actively involved in identifying and selecting topics and themes for projects, since he believed student interest and motivation would increase if children took part in planning their learning.

The project approach faded from the scene somewhat with the demise of the Progressive movement, but received renewed support once again in the 1950s as the works of Jean Piaget became familiar in educational circles. Piaget believed the child to be instrumental in bringing meaning and organization to his or her world by his interacting with the environment. That is, each child individually constructs his or her own unique reality through sensory experiences. In the classroom, he suggested, this development can be encouraged by student-centered, self-directed, hands-on activities, including integrated projects and learning centers. The integration of the various disciplines is a natural process in project learning, where children are encouraged to organize and construct knowledge in a holistic fashion, much as learning occurs in the "real" world.

In recent years, as interest in the constructivist movement has grown, so too has interest in the project approach to the curriculum. Projects allow students the opportunity to investigate and explore an area of interest, a question, or a problem rather than presenting predetermined activities and objectives. The child is, in a sense, able to pursue his own goals and learning. The project approach lends itself well to a constructivist philosophy, which holds that children create knowledge through their interactions with the social and physical environment. Projects, designed by teacher and student together, or by the student alone, provide an environment where interdisciplinary constructions and connections can be made, fostering conceptual development and understanding.

WHY USE A PROJECT APPROACH TO THE CURRICULUM?

When approaching the curriculum from an interdisciplinary perspective, one can find several reasons for choosing to use projects in the classroom.

APPLICATION OF KNOWLEDGE

When involved in project work, a child has the opportunity to apply learned knowledge. This is particularly true when the project is interdisciplinary in nature. For example, in a traditional, subject-oriented curriculum, the student is asked to "learn" (memorize) certain mathematical principles and concepts such as addition, percentage, and measurement. This learning, however, is often tied to textbooks and may not challenge or allow the student to actually use the knowledge in practical situations. The student may indeed have a textbook understanding of computing percentage or measuring with fractions, but may not be able to relate these ideas to real-life experiences or problems. A project, however, may necessarily require the student to calculate interest or sales tax, or measure materials in the context of solving a larger problem. Also, a project frequently integrates several disciplines, which requires students to apply knowledge and skills beyond the "prescribed" subject area. Math skills and concepts, for example, can be used in situations that extend beyond the math discipline , such as in baking, sewing, composing music, and the like. The opportunity to apply interdisciplinary knowledge and skills to practical situations, then, is an advantage of the project approach.

CONSIDERATION OF STUDENTS' INTERESTS

A second reason to consider using projects with an interdisciplinary curriculum is that students' interests and ideas can be taken into account when designing projects. A major tenet of the student-centered curriculum is that students are more highly motivated to take charge of their learning if they are allowed some input at the planning stage. Students whose interests and curiosity are captured by a particular subject, idea, problem, or question are more likely to be self-directed in carrying out the project, and hopefully in developing and refining knowledge, skills, and attitudes. And while a student may not particularly enjoy studying fractions or percentages in isolation, if these concepts are learned and practiced in the context of a project that he or she finds interesting, challenging, or motivating, they may be less threatening, less boring, or less confusing.

MAKING SCHOOL-TO-LIFE CONNECTIONS

A project approach, particularly one that attempts to weave together the various academic disciplines, allows the student to make connections between life in the classroom and life in the greater community. Real-life projects carried out in the classroom may well imitate situations and experiences that students can expect to find in their communities when they leave the school setting. For example, when students undertake a project to identify pollution levels in local water sources (streams, lakes, bays, rivers, etc.), and to determine the impact of this pollution on sea life, they are, in effect, undertaking the type of work that might be done by workers in a department of ecology. In this case, students would likely work together to gather and analyze data about sources, types, and effects of pollution, and to reach some conclusions about the state of the local water sources. Science, math, reading, and writing are all part of the effort to address a meaningful problem.

The school-to-life benefits of working on projects are not limited to the academic, however. In collaborating with other students, the child will necessarily develop a sense of community, as well as an understanding and appreciation for the democratic process. Working with others to accomplish a common task involves compromise, tolerance, participation, respect, and patience, all fundamental to a strong democracy. Thus, a project approach may assist the student in making connections between school and "real life" not only in terms of knowledge, but also in terms of social skills and citizenship development.

ADDRESSING THE INFORMATION REVOLUTION

In an age when knowledge seems to grow at an unprecedented pace, it is difficult for the teacher to know what to teach and what to eliminate from the curriculum. We are continually confronted with new information, including technological advances, medical breakthroughs, and scientific developments. Both teacher and students are directly impacted by the expansion of knowledge, in the form of state mandates regarding what must be taught. The addition of AIDS curriculum, drug and alcohol programs, sex education, personal safety programs, and environmental issues leave the teacher feeling that there is not enough time to teach "the basics." An interdisciplinary curriculum is one way to address the issue of information overload, as the walls between subjects are broken down. Knowledge and skills weaved together allow for some reduction in the overpowering amount of content that must be taught and learned.

INTEGRATION OF SUBJECT AREAS

Most important to the discussion of interdisciplinary curriculum is the potential of projects to bring together the various subject areas. Students, it is believed, are better able to organize and construct knowledge when it is experienced in a holistic manner. That is, the mind makes meaning when it can see relationships and make connections. Projects afford teachers and learners the opportunity to integrate content, since a well-designed project is rarely limited to one skill or subject area. Rather, in solving a larger problem or answering a complex question, the learner is called upon to develop new knowledge and skills in a variety of areas. A student may take an interest in investigating the modes of transportation and traffic patterns in the community, for example. A project such as this would likely involve a study of population maps, employment statistics, school locations and bus routes, public transportation information, freeway on and off ramps, etc.

It seems clear that the project approach holds promise in terms of carrying out an interdisciplinary curriculum. It allows children the opportunity to choose or influence the selection of topics, to apply knowledge and skills, to make connections between school and the greater community, and to approach a problem or question from an interdisciplinary perspective. Projects have the potential to:

- motivate students
- promote self-directed behaviors
- increase the use of creative, resourceful, and alternative methods of problem solving
- improve decision-making skills
- encourage cooperative work experiences
- stimulate higher level thinking
- relate classroom learning to "real-life" situations

CONSIDERATIONS IN DESIGNING A SUCCESSFUL PROJECT

Whether students are given free reign in choosing a subject of study, or whether they work together with teachers, there are considerations that must be taken into account if the work is to be a successful learning experience for students. These considerations include the choice of a topic, problem, or question; methods that might be used in gathering information; availability of resources and materials; format for presentation of results; and assessment procedures.

Selection of a Topic, Problem, or Question. The first step in developing a project is the selection of a topic. Careful evaluation of questions, problems, and topics may well determine the eventual success of the experience. One of the most important considerations in deciding on the focus of a project is the students and their interests. The teacher must decide whether each student will have an individual project, whether the class will work on projects in cooperative groups, or whether the project will be designed for the entire class. This decision will vary depending on the individual teacher's willingness to include students in curriculum planning. Some teachers may be uncomfortable opening up curriculum design to students, which may limit students to suggesting only general areas of study. Other teachers, however, may be quite comfortable in sharing project design with students, and may allow the class to be part of the entire planning process. Certainly if each student is allowed the opportunity to design his or her own project, the matter of interest and motivation will be addressed. This approach does entail a great deal of organization on the part of the teacher, however, in that he or she must be the facilitator / monitor of 25–30 individual project studies. A whole-class project, on the other hand, may involve less organization and tracking on the part of the teacher, but is less likely to be motivating and of interest to each and every student in the class. The teacher must decide which option best fits his or her own needs, the needs of the students, and the specific time restraints of the situation. Either way, it is suggested that projects in some way reflect the interests and needs of the students. Selection of project topics should be driven by those subjects, questions, and problems that are relevant to students' lives.

In his book *Starting from Scratch: One Classroom Builds Its Own Curriculum,* Steven Levy discusses several projects he developed with elementary students (1996). He suggests six elements to consider when generating ideas for a project-based curriculum. These include:

- letting the curriculum emerge from the activity and experiences that occur naturally in the classroom and school community
- the importance of the interdisciplinary nature of project work
- the need for community buy-in and involvement
- the idea that projects should have real meaning to the students (Levy, 1996, p.34)

Projects, Levy maintains, come from "asking the right questions" (1996, p. 35). One question he asked, "What is the Ideal Classroom?" led to a year-long project in which students designed their classroom from the ground up. This included the raising of money for the supplies needed to build desks and chairs (Levy, 1996). In addition to the ideal classroom, projects emerged from questions such as "Why are our Shoes Made on the Other Side of the World?", "What is the Greatest Number?", and "How Did our Town Get Its Name?" (Levy, 1996).

The Interdisciplinary / Collaborative Nature of the Project. When deciding on a project focus, the teacher is wise to keep in mind the benefits of curriculum integration, and choose a problem, question, or topic that necessitates bringing together several different but related content areas. While a project dealing exclusively with math or science may indeed be of interest to students, the students will reap greater benefits if the project requires them to make connections between the different subjects, and to use skills from various disciplines. The scope of the project must be comprehensive enough, such that interdisciplinary study and connection naturally occur in the context of completing the project.

In addition to selecting a project that is interdisciplinary in nature, those that necessitate collaboration through in-depth investigation and problem solving will, as discussed earlier, lend themselves well to cooperative work and group investigation. This builds a sense of community and resolve, and fosters in children those collaborative skills they will need in future work situations.

The Structure of the Project. When designing an interdisciplinary project, the teacher must decide on the amount of structure to be built into the experience. An unstructured project is one where the student:

- takes an active role in selecting the topic, problem, or question for investigation
- develops a plan for completing the project

- works independently to secure information and materials
- decides on format of final product or conclusions to be presented

A structured project, on the other hand, has more teacher input in terms of topic identification, objectives / outcome, plan of action, and presentation of results. While students may have a voice in the generation and selection of a topic, the project is not wide open, but rather has certain parameters to guide its completion.

Adequacy of Resources. When deciding on a project topic, the teacher must keep in mind the types of resources that will be necessary to carry out the project, and the relative ease or difficulty that might be encountered in securing those resources. If paper supplies are necessary, can they be supplied by the school, or will students be expected to provide their own? Library resources should be reserved and/or secured ahead of time so that there are enough current, quality items available for in-depth study. If students are expected to contact members of the community in completing their project, the teacher should know that these people are available and *willing* to be contacted by students. Availability of computers for information searches and communication should be arranged as well. Finally, if site visits, field trips, or other travel arrangements are necessary components of the project, arrangements should be made well ahead of time.

Collection of Data. Once the teacher and students have decided on the focus of the project, the investigation begins! If the project has an unstructured design, the student takes responsibility for gathering and analyzing necessary information. If the project is to follow a more structured design, the teacher will act as facilitator and provide an environment suitable for gathering and analyzing information. In either case, this part of the project will likely be the most time-intensive, as students work to gather, share, and analyze information needed to solve the problem, answer the questions, or investigate the subject they have selected to study. Making and checking predictions, discussing ideas and findings, reflecting on the investigative process, and revising plans are all part of the "work" of projects. Ultimately, this work will result in some sort of product, report, or performance that reflects the knowledge, skills, and attitudes developed as a result of the study. These culminating experiences are helpful in bringing closure of the project, as much time and energy have been devoted to its completion.

ASTRONOMY AND THE PROJECT APPROACH

Let us assume for the sake of example that a teacher is planning a unit on astronomy for sixth grade students. This curriculum is mandated by the school district, and so there is a teacher's guide, some activities, and resources to support those activities. However, the teacher would like to allow students the opportunity to explore astronomy and all its related issues based on their own interests. In so doing the teacher hopes they will develop research and organizational skills, as well as the ability to connect the principles of astronomy with other areas of the curriculum. The teacher and students together brainstorm areas of interest that relate to the overarching theme of astronomy. Included in their suggestions might be such topics as the viability of moon colonies, early space travel, shuttle expeditions, telescopes, constellations, alien life forms, the planets, and black holes. Students choose individually or in small groups an idea or topic they would like to pursue in the form of a project. The teacher has secured numerous resources to support the projects, including computers programs, reference materials, films, maps and charts, and speakers. Throughout the projects, the teacher acts as a facilitator, monitoring progress, offering suggestions, evaluating the process, and giving encouragement. Students are responsible for developing a plan of action and carrying out the plan. The fact that astronomy and other curricular units are mandated or directed by the local school district need not limit the teacher in planning and implementing interdisciplinary projects. Rather, these topics may serve as the starting point for launching student projects. Required curricular units, such as astronomy, sea life, machines, patterns, the Pilgrims, economic supply and demand, life cycles, and health awareness are excellent subjects for use with projects. The big questions that can emerge from discussion of these topics can be the beginning of stimulating and informative interdisciplinary experiences.

CONCLUSION

In approaching the curriculum through interdisciplinary projects, students learn holistically, gaining an understanding of how subjects are connected in real life. When students are involved in a project approach to learning, they have the *time and freedom* to fully explore areas of interest. They take part in designing the curriculum, choosing topics that are relevant and motivating. In planning, researching, and reporting on a problem or question, children develop cognitive processes. Also, when students collaborate on project work, they are developing social skills, leading to social competence. Project learning, then, reflects a constructivist view of learning, where students build their own understanding through exploration and reflection. Both academic and social skills are developed in an environment that encourages active, interdisciplinary, self-directed learning.

USING THEMES IN AN INTERDISCIPLINARY CURRICULUM

A second approach to interdisciplinary teaching and learning is through theme-based units. In this approach, a theme, in the form of an overarching concept, is selected, and serves as a framework for the purpose of integrating the curriculum. Themes such as "Explorations," "Conflict and Change," "Discoveries," "Patterns," "Survival," and "Why Man Creates" are the "big ideas" around which knowledge, skills, and attitudes can be developed. Integrating the curriculum around themes is supported for some of the same reasons that are given for teaching with projects.

First, students are better able to organize and create knowledge when it is experienced not as separate subjects or bits of information, but in a larger context, such that they can see relationships and connections. Secondly, a curriculum integrated around a larger theme or concept is more representative of how we experience real life. Whether we are accomplishing work-related tasks or attempting to solve the problems and questions associated with daily life, we often pull together knowledge and skills from various "subject" areas. Curricular experiences that encourage thinking and problem solving in an integrated fashion prepare us for dealing with real-life situations. A theme based approach also has the advantage of creating a sense of community, as the entire class shares in gathering information, solving problems, and answering questions dealing with a common theme. The opportunities to work collaboratively, to negotiate and compromise, and to practice patience and respect can be built into a theme-based unit, fostering citizenship development.

A third consideration is that of student interest and motivation to learn. Theme-based instruction, like interdisciplinary projects, can be designed from a student-centered perspective, taking into account students' needs and interests. When students are involved in choosing and planning their learning experiences, they are more likely to have a personal interest in carrying out the identified activities and tasks.

Finally, it is suggested that theme-based teaching and learning is helpful in reducing the ever-increasing amount of information with which we are faced. The information revolution leaves teachers in the uncomfortable position of having to decide and choose what information can realistically be added to an already full curriculum. Using theme-based instruction to integrate the various disciplines allows teachers to combine content in an attempt to reduce the overwhelming amount of information.

A theme-based approach to interdisciplinary studies, then, offers students the opportunity to organize and construct knowledge in the context of an overarching concept, identifying relationships and making connections. Also, it is an approximation of real life, in that problems, questions, and tasks presented by the theme are approached in a holistic manner. Themes also provide an avenue for combining and reducing the amount of information teachers must attempt to teach.

DEVELOPING A SUCCESSFUL THEME UNIT

When creating theme-based units of instruction, thorough preparation and planning will do much to assure a successful learning experience for students. Considerations to be addressed when designing units include:

- choosing a theme
- writing unit outcomes
- making connections between the theme and the various content areas
- choosing or developing activities
- developing an assessment plan

Choosing a Theme of Study. The first step in creating a theme-based unit of instruction is to identify an area suitable for study. This can be done by the teacher or by a team of teachers, or it can be done jointly with students. In either case, a brainstorming session to identify possible themes is suggested. When considering themes, several factors need to be taken into account. The first of these is student interest. A theme should be one that captures the interest and curiosity of students if it is to be motivating and challenging. Student involvement in the initial brainstorming can be most helpful in determining which subjects (topics) stimulate curiosity and interest. Another factor to consider when selecting a theme is the scope of the topic. "Apples," "Bears," "Pumpkins," and "Whales" may well be themes that are of interest to teacher and students, but may or may not be of sufficient scope to provoke challenging questions or problems, or may not get at higher level thinking outcomes. On the other hand, complex themes such as "Cultures," "Diversity," or "Bias" may be inappropriate or difficult to implement.

Finally, it is necessary when choosing a theme to assess the resources that will be necessary for the activities to be carried out completely and successfully. Whether there is a need for supplies, travel, speakers, technology, or literature, the teacher must be cognizant of the availability of resources and how they will be accessed.

A summary of guidelines to consider when planning an interdisciplinary unit are as follows:

- Choose a suitable theme, for example, "night," "places," "construction," "creation," "free time," "invention," "discovery," etc.
- Bring the class together for a discussion of possibilities.
- Establish center or focal points of learning.
- Post a list of differentiated activities related to the topic.
- Develop strategies for involving the home.
- Create a relaxed, informal atmosphere.
- Share information daily on the topic of study.
- Meet with students to set and reflect on personal goals.
- Encourage freedom, creativity, and discovery.
- Encourage students to work together.
- Allow time for student sharing.
- Involve resource people such as librarians, artists, professional people, service groups, etc.
- Encourage students to present their work for others, including students, parents, civic groups, and retirement homes.
- Emphasize reflective, responsible techniques for evaluation.

Writing Outcomes. After a theme has been selected, the teacher must determine outcomes for the unit of study; that is, what is it that the students will be expected to know and do at the completion of the unit? Outcomes may reflect academic content, skills, behaviors, and /or attitudes. Content outcomes may be guided by district expectations, but may also be developed from questions raised by the theme itself. For example, what questions are posed by a theme such as "War and Peace"? Possibilities include:

- Where have major wars taken place in the world?
- How has war changed over the past five centuries?
- What are those issues that have led to war?
- Historically, how has peace been achieved?
- Have (how have) attitudes to peace and war changed over the years?

Questions that might direct a theme-based unit on "The Westward Movement" include:

- What was it that drew people to leave their homes and move west?
- Who were the people that migrated west?
- What hardships were involved in moving and settling in the west?
- How did the Indians perceive the Westward Movement?
- What role did weather play in the Westward Movement?

Once several guiding questions have been identified, they can be used to determine the content outcomes of the unit. For the unit on "The Westward Movement," content would include a study of miners, farmers, cattle ranchers, cattle drives, geography of the middle states, Indian settlements and lifestyle, etc.

Connecting the Theme to the Outcomes. After determining outcomes of the unit, the teacher can begin to create a unit web, which is a visual "map" of how the various content areas can be effectively integrated to support the chosen theme. Depending on the scope and focus of the theme, two, three, or even more disciplines might be identified as having logical connections to the theme. Not every subject will lend itself to integration with every theme; it is better to integrate only those areas that naturally support and complement the theme, rather than to try and integrate every subject with every theme. Forcing illogical or unnatural content integration diminishes the value of interdisciplinary study, as the concept or subject loses its focus.

An example of a theme web is shown in Figure 3.1. Marine life is the topic to be studied in this particular unit, intended for a third grade classroom. Science, math, the arts, social studies, and language arts have been identified as subjects that could be effectively integrated to support the theme. With this framework established, the teacher is ready to move to the next step in developing a theme unit.

FIGURE 3.1 INTERDISCIPLINARY THEME: MARINE LIFE

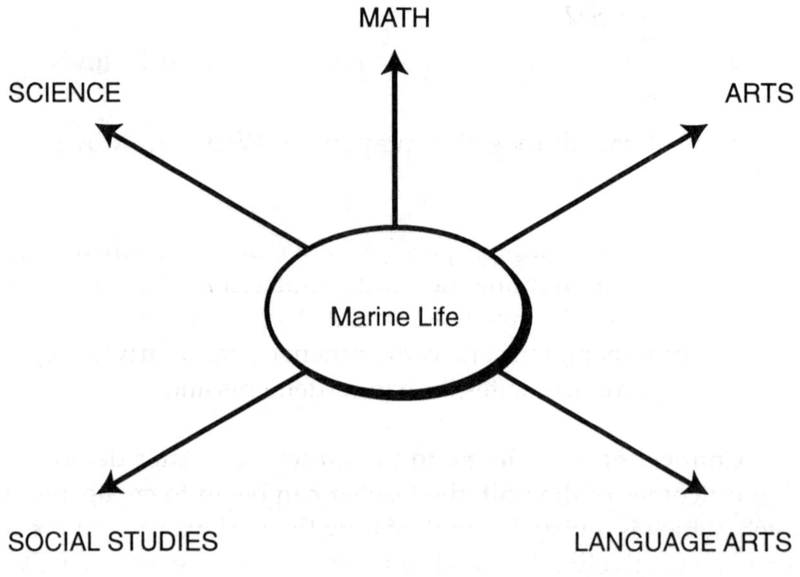

Selecting Activities. Teachers next must select or develop activities that not only connect subject areas together, but also connect subjects to the overall theme. In the unit on marine life, for example, science experiments involving fresh and salt water (pollution levels, food chains, etc.) would connect science, math, and health content to the theme. In addition to selecting activities that connect the curriculum to the theme, the teacher should plan activities that reflect the different levels of the cognitive, affective, and psychomotor domains. Students should be asked not only to study the theme at a factual level, but to analyze, synthesize, and evaluate information and issues related to marine life. When selecting activities, the teacher must constantly refer back to the unit outcomes and objectives to ensure that each activity in some way supports those outcomes and objectives (What do I want my students to *know* at the end of the unit?). Too often, according to Erickson (1993, p. 9), "we stop with the activity and fail to reach relevant closure with students."

Another example of a theme plan is shown in Figure 3.2. The proposed unit focuses on land and environment, and was developed for students in the primary grades (Godwin-Austen, 1995). In planning the unit, the teacher first identified content areas that provide a good fit with the theme, including science, social studies, math, music and art, and the language arts. Next the teacher developed or selected activities within each subject area that logically support and integrate the theme of land and environment. In science, for example, the students will conduct an experiment dealing with the effects of pollution on plant growth. Results of experiments within the classroom may be generalized to the greater environment, so that students develop an awareness of the detrimental effects of pollution on our land. (See Figure 3.3.) In addition, students will keep a "weather journal" of cities from across the country for the purpose of comparing climatic conditions of different geographic locales. These results will be graphed for visual comparison purposes.

Social studies activities include identifying natural resources unique to the Pacific Northwest, as well as those dealing with mapping concepts and skills. In learning about natural resources, students may write letters to Chambers of Commerce across the state to gather "data" about natural resources, thereby integrating language and social studies.

FIGURE 3.2 INTERDISCIPLINARY THEME: MARINE LIFE

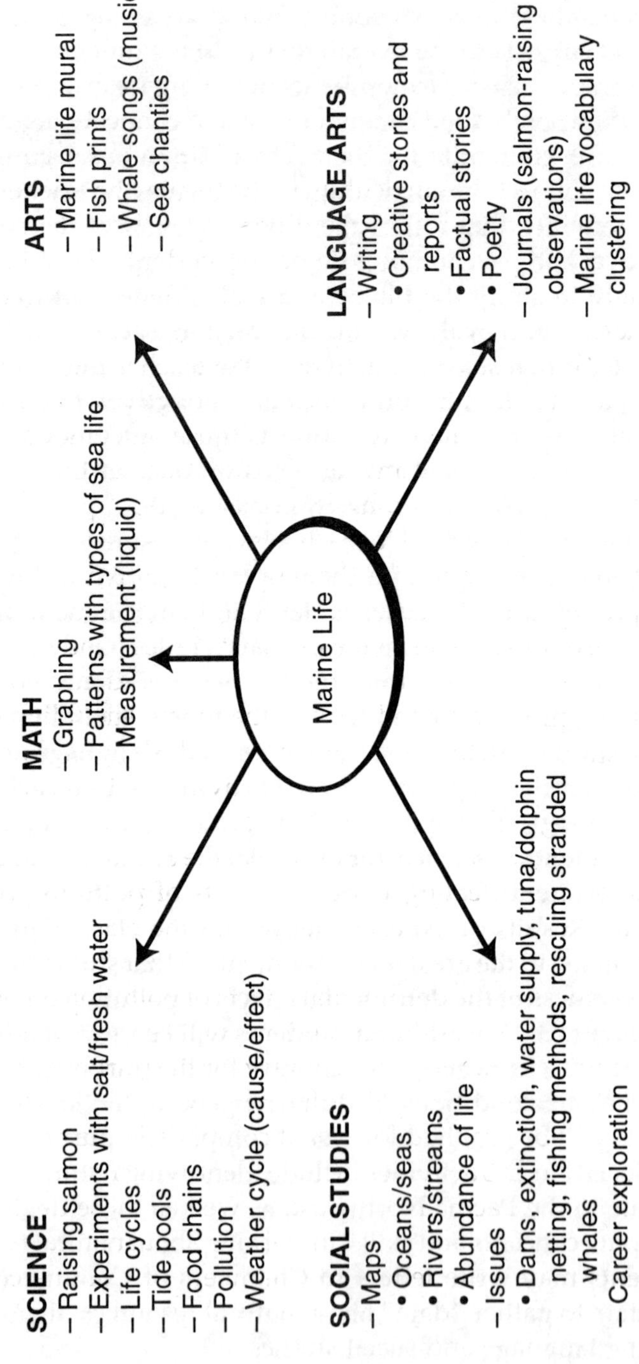

Finally, the teacher has identified culminating activities to be undertaken at the end of the unit. Students will put into practice some of their knowledge about pollution and the environment during a field trip to clean up a local creek or lake. They will also design some type of conservation plan for their home or for the school. Lastly, students will be given a test to determine the extent to which they mastered content covered by the unit.

Assessment of the Unit. Finally, the teacher must put together some type of assessment plan which can be used to demonstrate students' mastery of the unit outcomes. The plan should include criteria for assessing knowledge, skills, and behaviors. Assessment might include a formative component, including portfolio work and ongoing evaluation, or a combination of both formative and summative assessments, including pen and paper tests and performance tasks. In addition, many teachers choose to conclude theme-based units with a culminating activity, such as a science fair, a play, or a field trip.

Themes, then, are a way to approach an interdisciplinary curriculum that allow the student to make connections between subjects to an overarching concept or idea. Through theme-based instruction, teachers can offer students the opportunity to explore relevant subject matter in depth, to develop higher order thinking skills, and to make connections between school and the "real" world.

TEAM TEACHING

Team teaching is a strategy that may be employed in the implementation of an interdisciplinary curriculum. Teaming can be defined as the work undertaken by two or more teachers in planning, implementing, and assessing the curriculum. This partnership may take one of several forms, but generally serves to allow a group of teachers the opportunity to share their knowledge and skills in integrating the curriculum in order to provide positive, *connected* learning experiences for students.

FIGURE 3.3 PLANNING WEB

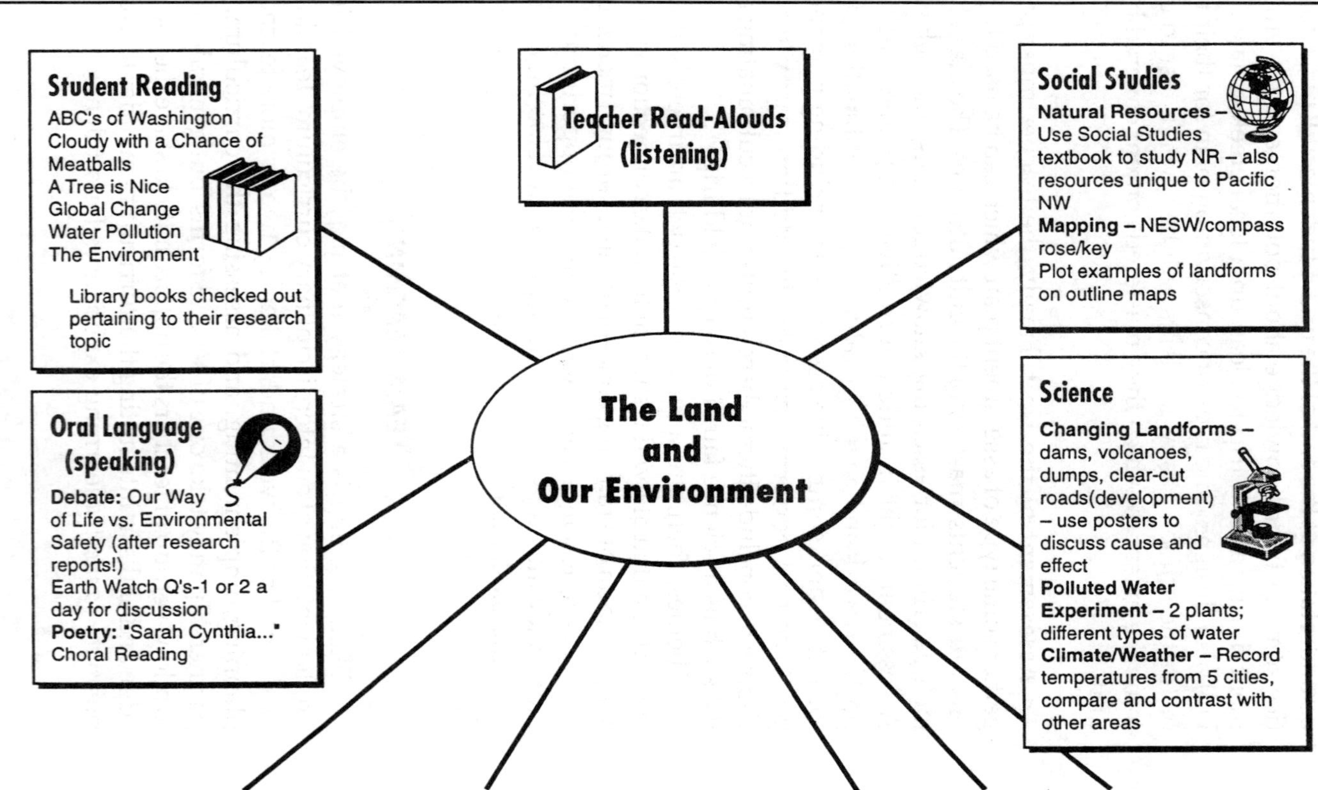

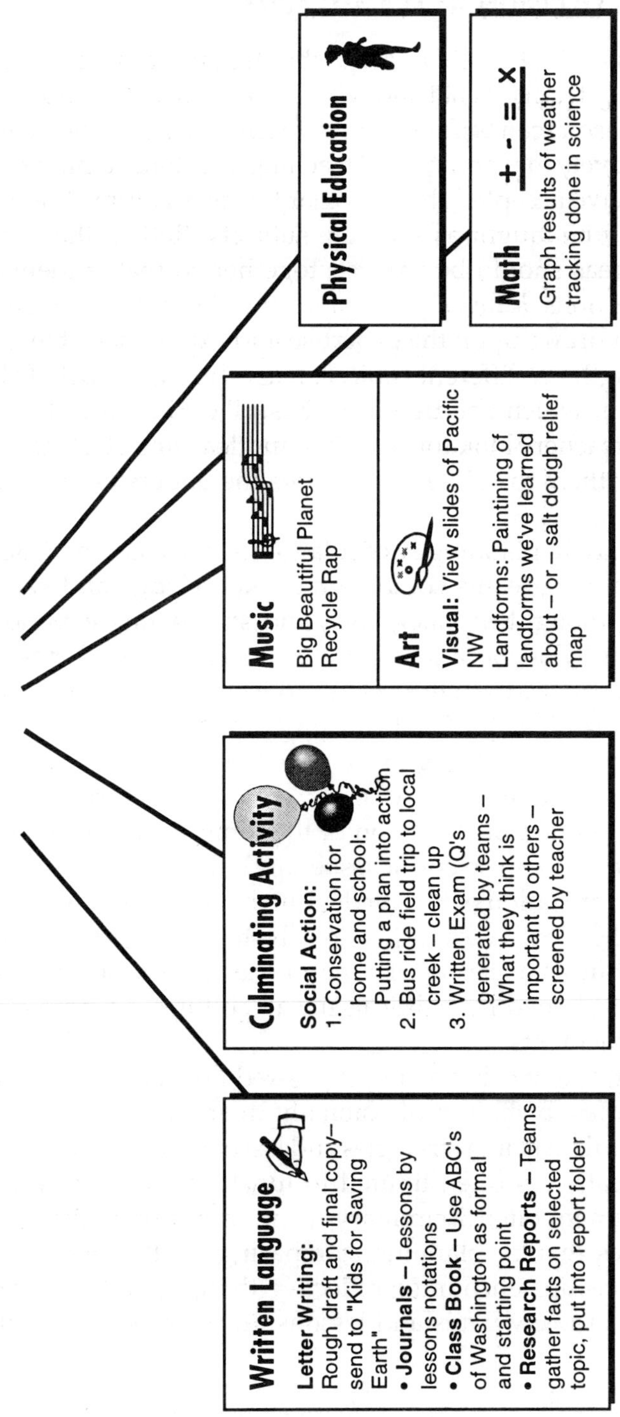
Written Language
Letter Writing:
Rough draft and final copy–send to "Kids for Saving Earth"
• Journals – Lessons by lessons notations
• Class Book – Use ABC's of Washington as formal and starting point
• Research Reports – Teams gather facts on selected topic, put into report folder
Culminating Activity
Social Action:
1. Conservation for home and school: Putting a plan into action
2. Bus ride field trip to local creek – clean up
3. Written Exam (Q's generated by teams – What they think is important to others – screened by teacher
Music
Big Beautiful Planet
Recycle Rap
Art
Visual: View slides of Pacific NW
Landforms: Paintining of landforms we've learned about – or – salt dough relief map
Physical Education
Math
+ - = x
Graph results of weather tracking done in science

WHY THE DECISION TO TEAM TEACH?

Why is it that teachers make the decision to work in interdisciplinary teams? What and whose needs are being addressed? Several reasons can be found. First, teachers who choose to work collaboratively in planning and teaching an interdisciplinary curriculum have accepted the idea that the curriculum should not necessarily be taught as separate subjects. Rather, the various content areas should be weaved together so that students see the connections *between* and *within* the disciplines. Team collaboration draws upon the expertise and experience of teachers with strengths in different subject areas who share a belief about the ways in which children learn best. Working from this perspective, teachers look for teaching and learning strategies that best allow them to deliver or facilitate the understanding of the curriculum.

Secondly, in planning curricular units, activities, and assessments, teaching teams combine their knowledge and skills in designing thoughtful, integrated, and stimulating experiences for students. Collaboration seems to foster increased creativity and insight in ways that working in isolation does not. In approaching a unit on the Civil War, for example, history, language, and science teachers bring to the table their unique understandings of that time period. As they work together, the teachers develop a unified presentation of the topic, tying together historical, literary, and scientific issues and events. This interdisciplinary organization of the curriculum benefits students, in that they see the Civil War not just as a historical event—a date in history—but as a period of time in the history of our nation which was shaped by political, social, cultural, economic, and scientific incidents.

Finally, teachers have long expressed the need for increased opportunities to share professionally their successful (and not so successful) teaching strategies and lessons. While professional communication is often limited to lunch conversations in the faculty lounge, interdisciplinary teaming not only allows, but necessitates regular planning, comparing, and sharing. Teaming relationships encourage reflective thought and discussion, as teachers review plans and lessons. In the process of reflecting together on teaching and learning situations, teams of teachers can analyze, clarify, and rethink classroom situations and experiences, leading to confirmation or change of previously held ideas or practices. Vygotsky (1978) pointed out the relationship between learning and social interactions. Engaging in reflective dialogue with team members allows teachers to develop and refine their ideas about teaching and learning, which in turn may lead to improvement in the planning and implementation of interdisciplinary curriculum.

HOW DOES TEAMING WORK?

Teacher teams may be formed in several different ways, and may take on different forms. Merenbloom (1996) describes three types of teams, two of which are relevant to our discussion of interdisciplinary studies. An *interdisciplinary team* is one in which four or five teachers of different subject areas jointly plan instructional experiences for their four or five classes of students. Each brings his or her subject expertise, and together they integrate content such that the student is exposed to a curriculum where relationships and connections are purposefully identified and taught. Drake recommends that "as many different subject areas as possible be involved in curriculum building. It may seem time consuming, but it really helps everyone to begin to see and think in terms of interconnections" (1991, p. 22). In secondary situations, this might mean that history, language, science, math, and teachers of the arts join together to explore curricular connections or to plan interdisciplinary units of study. In elementary schools, teachers with different interests and strengths may decide to form teams, pooling their knowledge and skills to do interdisciplinary planning and teaching.

A second type of team (Merenbloom, 1996) is the *combination team*, or mini-interdisciplinary team. This is a team made up of two teachers of different subjects who integrate their curriculum, and teach the same double class (60–75 students) for a two-period block of time. For example, a high school social studies teacher and English teacher may team to integrate American History and Literature. Rather than being taught in isolation, the teachers plan the curriculum such that historical events and literature complement and reinforce each other, all the while clarifying the social, political, and economic connections of the time. Combination teams are also found in the elementary school, where two teachers collaborate to develop interdisciplinary units of study. In either case, the aim is a more connected, holistic learning experience for students.

Team teaching, then, is one strategy that can be effectively used in planning, teaching, and assessing an interdisciplinary curriculum. Working collaboratively to connect subjects and topics, to map the curriculum, and to develop interdisciplinary units and activities, teachers "help students see the totality of learning" (Merenbloom, 1996, p. 49).

COOPERATIVE LEARNING

Cooperative learning, where students work in small groups to accomplish a particular academic goal, "has been suggested as the solution for an astonishing array of educational problems: it is often cited as a means of emphasizing thinking skills and increasing higher-order learning; as an alternative to ability grouping, remediation, or special education; as a means of improving race relations and acceptance of mainstreamed students; and as a way to prepare students for an increasingly collaborative work force" (Slavin, 1991, p. 82). Whether or not cooperative learning is a model that can effectively address these issues is not certain. It does seem clear, however, that the model has much to offer teachers and students engaged in interdisciplinary study. Joyce, Weil and Showers (1992), in discussing the model, suggest that a synergy is generated in cooperative learning situations, such that motivation is increased over what it would be in isolated, individualistic learning situations. The sense of community achieved in cooperative groups produces positive energy. This is a plus.

In addition to the positive energy and motivation generated by cooperative learning groups, they have the effect of encouraging children to learn from and to teach each other. In a recent study done to determine the effects of peer tutoring on seventh grade students, it was noted that ". . . strategies using a collaborative teaching approach and peer tutoring have shown promise for decreasing school drop-out rates and increasing academic achievement" (Roswell et al., 1995, p. 275). The social interactions that occur during cooperative group work are examples of instances where language impacts cognitive development. In planning, organizing, carrying out, and discussing their work with one another, students generate cognitive and social complexity, creating intellectual activity that may indeed increase learning (Joyce, Weil, & Showers, 1992).

Finally, the social interactions that result from cooperative group work give children the opportunity for reflective thought, as they consider, analyze, hypothesize, and rethink the ways in which they attempt to solve problems, answer questions, and accomplish tasks (Joyce, Weil, & Showers, 1992). Donald Schon, who observed professional business people in their work, has written about the value of reflection in problem solving. He noted that adults, in routinely carrying out their work, rely not only on knowledge and skills, but also on the art of reflection. That is, in the process of solving a problem, we often reflect on the process in which we are involved: what we have accomplished so far, where we stand, and what steps must be taken to complete the task. It has been argued by Dewey and others that reflective thought is valuable not only to working adults, but also to children as they solve the problems of the curriculum. Cooperative learning models offer children the chance to reflect with their peers as they work together on classroom projects and activities.

Cooperative learning groups, then, are thought to generate synergy, motivation, peer teaching and learning, greater levels of complex intellectual activity, and reflective thought. Any one of these outcomes would be advantageous in implementing an interdisciplinary curriculum. Projects and theme-based units, which are frequently used in interdisciplinary studies, rely heavily on motivation, peer interactions, higher level thinking, and reflective thought, suggesting that cooperative groups should be an integral part of interdisciplinary planning.

COOPERATIVE LEARNING METHODS: GROUP INVESTIGATION

The principle of cooperative learning, as we have noted, is "small groups of students working together to help each other learn academic material" (Slavin, 1991, p. 82). There are several cooperative learning methods that have found success including STL (student team learning), Jigsaw, Learning Together, and Group Investigation. While all might be effectively used in different educational situations, group investigation seems particularly well-suited to interdisciplinary studies.

Group investigation is a cooperative learning method in which students form groups based on their interest in a particular topic for in-depth study and investigation. Group inquiry, discussion, and projects are central to this learning model. Students are actively involved in planning *what* they will study and *how* they will study it. They work collaboratively to develop a research plan and then divide the work among group members. At the conclusion of the project, group members prepare individual and / or a group presentation to share their results and conclusions. Given that projects are frequently used in interdisciplinary studies, the advantages of using this model seems clear. Student input into topic selection and planning, active involvement, self-directed behaviors, and discussion are all necessary components of project work, and are afforded by group investigation.

STAGES OF GROUP INVESTIGATION

Sharan and Sharan, who developed the group investigation model, outline six stages of group investigation that students move through in carrying out their study (1989–90, p. 37). These stages include:

- Identification of the topic of study/formation of groups
- Planning the group investigation
- Carrying out the investigation
- Preparation of the final report/product
- Report Presentation
- Evaluation

I. Identification of the topic of study / formation of groups.

1. Whether the topic is part of the mandated curriculum, or whether it emerges from student interest, it should be broad enough in scope that it supports a variety of projects. It is suggested that the topic be framed as a questions (Sharan & Sharan, 1989–90) rather than as statements, to set the stage for inquiry and investigation. Examples of such general topic questions are: "Why Does Man Create?", "How Do We Get Our Food?", etc.
2. Students brainstorm subtopics for project inquiry. After the general topic has been determined, students are asked to identify an area they would like to explore in depth. Sharan & Sharan (1989–90) suggest that each student develop a list of guiding questions that would warrant investigation. As students come together in small groups, and later as a class, the list of questions is consolidated such that the final set of questions represents the interests of all students.
3. Questions are made available to each student for consideration.
4. Questions are categorized and presented as subtopics for group investigation.
5. Subtopics are titled and students form cooperative groups based on their interest in the subtopics.

II. Planning the group investigation

1. At this stage, students meet in their groups to begin planning. The first step is to formulate a more specific problem or question for investigation; that is, if the general topic is "How Do We Get Our Food?", a group of students may choose a subtopic dealing with farming, food processing, marketing, shipping, etc.
2. Next, students decide on ways to research or study the problem. What information will be needed, how will it be gathered, and what will be done with it once gathered?

3. Finally, the topic is divided into manageable pieces and group members identify that piece on which they will focus their attention.

III. Carrying out the investigation

Each member of the group follows through with his or her part of the plan. Each day begins with a review of what is to be accomplished that day.

IV. Preparation of the final report / product

As the investigations near their end, students come back together in their groups to compile information into a culminating presentation of what they have learned. The teacher is facilitator, giving input as to whether presentations are appropriate and "doable."

V. Report Presentation

The class once again gathers as a whole, and each group makes the presentation of its project findings.

VI. Evaluation

While the teacher will usually make a final evaluation of each group's project, the reality of group investigation is that evaluation occurs throughout the entire process, both by the teacher and by the students. The teacher, as facilitator, offers daily feedback on the work and progress of each group. Students, in their investigations and discussions, are involved in continual reflection and evaluation as they analyze and refine their ideas, plans, and actions. Both formative and summative assessments are components of the group investigation model of teaching and learning.

CONCLUSION

Group investigation, then, is a useful strategy in interdisciplinary studies in that it allows students the opportunity to conduct in-depth investigations into areas of interest. These investigations are not limited to a single subject area, but instead require students to answer a question or solve a problem using skills and information from across disciplines. In doing this, children see the natural connections between subjects, just as we see and experience those connections in our everyday lives.

REFERENCES

Bodrova, E. & Leong, D. (1996). *Tools of the mind: The Vygotskian approach to early childhood education.* Edgewood Cliffs, NJ: Prentice-Hall.

DeVries, R., & Zan, B. (1994). *Moral classrooms, moral children: Creating a constructivist atmosphere in early education.* New York: Teachers College Press.

Dixon-Krauss, L. (1996). *Vygotsky in the classroom: Mediated literacy instruction and assessment.* New York: Longman.

Drake, S. (1991). How our team dissolved the boundaries. *Educational Leadership,* October, pp. 20–22.

Erickson, L. (1993). Integrating the curriculum: Procedures and pitfalls. *Curriculum in Context.* Fall/Winter, p. 7–9.

Five, C.L. & Dionisio. M. (1996). *Bridging the gap: Integrating curriculum in upper elementary and middle schools.* Portsmouth, NH: Heinemann.

Fogarty, R. (1994). Thinking about themes: Hundreds of themes. *Middle School Journal,* March, pp. 30–31.

Fraze, B., & Rudnitski, R. (1995). *Integrated teaching methods.* Albany, NY: Delmar Publishers.

Godwin-Austen, M. (1995). Unpublished interdisciplinary planning web.

Henry, J. (1994). *Teaching through projects.* London: Kogan Page Ltd.

Johnson, J., Carlson, S., Kastl, J., & Kastl, R. (1992). Developing conceptual thinking: The concept attainment model. *The Clearing House, 66,* (2), pp. 117–121.

Joyce, B. & Weil, M. (1996). *Models of teaching.* Needham Heights, MA: Allyn & Bacon.

Joyce, B., Weil, M., & Showers, B. (1992). *Models of teaching.* Needham Heights, MA: Allyn & Bacon.

Levy, S. (1996). *Starting from scratch: One classroom builds its own curriculum*. Portsmouth, N.H.: Heinemann.

Merenbloom, E. (1996). Team teaching: Addressing the learning needs of middle level students. *NASSP Bulletin, 80* (578), pp. 45–53.

Roswell, G. M., et al. (1995). Effects of collaborative peer tutoring on urban seventh graders. *The Journal of Educational Research, 88,* (5), pp. 275–279.

Sharan, Y. & Sharan, S. (1989–90). Group investigation expands cooperative learning. *Educational Leadership, 47,* December–January, pp. 37–41.

Slavin, R. (1991). Synthesis of research on cooperative learning. *Educational Leadership, 48,* February, pp. 82–88.

Sutherland, P. (1992). *Cognitive development today: Piaget and his critics*. London: Paul Chapman Publishing.

Vygotsky, L.S. (1962). *Thought and language*. Cambridge, MA: MIT Press.

Vygotsky, L.S. (1978). *Mind and society: The development of higher mental processes*. Cambridge, MA: Harvard University Press. (Original work published in 1930, 1933, and 1935).

Wortham, S.C. (1996). *The integrated classroom: The assessment-curriculum link in early childhood education*. Edgewood Cliffs, NJ: Merrill Publishing.

4

Interdisciplinary Curriculum in the Schools: What Teachers Are Doing

As teachers venture into the field of interdisciplinary studies, they frequently have practical questions about the actual development and implementation of an integrated curriculum, the dynamics of team teaching, scheduling concerns, and the assessment of student work. Specifically, they want to know:

- How do teachers work together to develop an interdisciplinary curriculum?
- What themes or concepts are best suited for interdisciplinary studies?
- What is a reasonable time frame for an interdisciplinary unit?
- How is scheduling arranged for integrated studies?
- What are examples of activities that work well in interdisciplinary classes?
- How are interdisciplinary lessons and units assessed?

This chapter is an attempt to answer some of these questions, based on the experiences of teachers who have "been there and done that." Five interdisciplinary programs are reviewed here, including discussions of how teachers decided to move into interdisciplinary studies, themes and activities that have proved valuable, successes and challenges of interdisciplinary work, recommendations on how to best approach an interdisciplinary program, as well as samples of student work and a unit outline for an interdisciplinary unit.

While these programs have been designed specifically for middle and high school students, they could certainly be adapted to other grade levels. Each program review includes the name and phone number of a contact person, who is, in most cases, a developer of the program. These educators are enthusiastic supporters of interdisciplinary studies, and are most generous in sharing their experiences with others. In addition to these people, more information regarding interdisciplinary programs can be found in Chapter 5.

Rain Forests and Social Responsibility

Sixth Grade

When Butch Beedle and his colleagues began experimenting with team teaching and the development of integrated units six years ago, they were unaware that there was a name for these teaching strategies. Only later did they learn that they were part of the interdisciplinary movement. What they *were* sure of from the beginning, however, was that the idea of making purposeful connections between subjects was sound educational practice, and would be beneficial for their students. Since that time, the teachers at J.C. McKenna Middle School in Evansville, Wisconsin, have developed, implemented, and refined a number of interdisciplinary units. One of these is the nationally recognized unit titled *Rain Forests and Social Responsibility*.

McKenna's Rainforest unit has been taught since 1991 as an interdisciplinary unit. Five teachers of core classes — Social Studies, Reading, Language Arts, Math, and Science—collaborate to plan and implement the unit, with each teacher accepting responsibility for specific content and skills. Then in 1992, Beedle decided to augment the unit with a newspaper which tied together the various concepts, content, and skills, believing this would be a logical and useful culminating activity. Indeed, the *Tropical Tribune* has gone on to receive a grand prize from Prentice-Hall and the National Middle School Association as an outstanding team teaching project.

A Sampling of Activities

The Rain Forest unit begins, as do all their interdisciplinary units, with "bait," those activities designed to create background knowledge for students, to produce enthusiasm for the topic, and to motivate all types of learners. Examples of "bait" include guest speakers, plays, movies, field trips, music, stories, and the like.

Guest speakers are an important part of the rain forest unit. Researchers and environmentalists are invited to share their expertise with students on such topics as Amazon River dolphins, Howler monkeys, and the Yanomamo Indians. Besides presenting factual information, each guest also holds a mock press conference which gives students an opportunity to practice note-taking, technical writing skills, and recording direct quotes. These skills are in turn used in creating the *Tropical Tribune*.

In Language Arts, students do research on animals of the rain forest so that they can write their own fictional animal stories. In addition, Jill Schultz and Leslie Ferrell, the Language Arts and Reading team members, teach many of the skills needed to produce a newspaper during the seven-week unit, including interviewing techniques and the writing of lead paragraphs.

In Social Studies and Science, Butch Beedle and Larry Dobbs have students learn factual information about the rainforests as well as explore the social issues which surround endangered habitats. What are the rain forests, why are they important, what is happening to them, and what is being done to solve problems related to them? Those are just some of the questions the students attempt to answer. Kim Wallinger, the Math team member, also deals with rates of deforestation, as well as the mathematical dimensions of species extinction with an activity using different varieties of candy.

The students at J.C. McKenna have been fortunate to have "adopted" a scientist named Laura Marsh. Laura began working with students and teachers at McKenna when she was doing work on her Ph.D., researching Howler monkeys in Belize. During that time, she kept a journal of her work which she shared with McKenna students, and also sent them scientific questions and activities to enrich their rainforest study. In turn, the students have supplied schools in Belize with many of the materials they lack.

SUCCESSES AND CHALLENGES

The interdisciplinary team at McKenna has worked together for six years in developing a number of integrated units, including "Conflict/U.S. Civil War," "Survival/Western Expansion," "The American Dream/Immigration/Industrial Revolution," "Equality/Civil Rights," as well as the Rainforest/Social Responsibility unit. Their successes have encouraged and given direction to colleagues who are moving toward interdisciplinary studies. Specifically, the team found that:

- Teacher relationships have been strengthened.
- Students' sense of success, pride, and accomplishment have improved.
- Students work well cooperatively in non-contrived settings.
- Retention of material is greater.
- The *Tropical Tribune* is a highly motivational activity that leads to quality work.
- The award-winning newspaper has been a source of school and community pride.
- Teachers involved in interdisciplinary studies are totally committed to developing and teaching sound, coherent integrated units.

While successes have led to an extension of the interdisciplinary approach, there have also been challenges.

- The teachers find that there is never enough time to do all the planning, creating, implementing, and assessing that needs to be done.
- Scheduling has been a challenge, as teachers, staff, and administration work to devise time schedules which lend themselves to team teaching and an interdisciplinary curriculum.
- Money is an issue, in that there is no "loose money" in the budget to use when new, exciting opportunities arise.
- Logical connections cannot always be made for every subject in every unit, so when teachers find a connection to be too much of a stretch, they leave it alone.

- Finding age-appropriate reading materials for each theme and unit is difficult and time-consuming.
- Staying together, in terms of time, is a challenge when teaching an interdisciplinary curriculum.

Assessment of the interdisciplinary curriculum has been particularly challenging. The sixth grade interdisciplinary team at McKenna has developed a working assessment strategy, although team members continually look for ways to revise or improve it. As students move through a given interdisciplinary unit, each team member tests and evaluates students in their own subject area. These evaluations and grades make up a considerable portion of a student's final course grade. In addition to these evaluations, however, each student is required to complete an interdisciplinary project at the end of every unit. Team members have generated approximately 100 project ideas from which the students may choose, and these project ideas are grouped in categories such as written reports, musical projects, artistic projects, news broadcasts, fictional diaries, etc. Students must make their project selection from a different category each time, thereby expanding their "performance horizons."

Evaluation of the projects is done by the interdisciplinary team, with each member taking on approximately 20 projects. Assessment is done with the aid of a rubric written by the team. If students disagree with the score they receive, they may appeal the decision and ask for a meeting of the entire team to review the project and the evaluation decision. As with the development and implementation of an interdisciplinary curriculum, the assessment process is reviewed and revised continually in an ongoing effort to find best practice.

Despite these challenges, teachers and students have been pleased with the results of their interdisciplinary teaming. Students seem to have greater ownership in their learning as they participate in authentic, important tasks. This ownership, in turn, results not only in quality work, but also in an excitement and curiosity about the world that was not evident with the traditional curriculum. The teachers at McKenna continue to refine and add to their interdisciplinary curriculum in the belief that an integrated curriculum affords students a sound, connected learning experience.

Reproduced on the following pages are several examples from this project.

Contact:
Butch Beedle
J.C. McKenna Middle School, Evansville, Wisconsin
608-882-4780

FIGURE 4.1 THE *TROPICAL TRIBUNE*

The Tropical Tribune

The sixth grade students at J.C. McKenna Middle School have been studying tropical rainforests since 1988. They became one of the first groups of students in Wisconsin to purchase rainforest acres to protect endangered habitats. Through the print and television media, the actions of the students became a positive role model for other students wanting to save endangered forests. As student leadership and involvement grew, buying acres of rainforest did not seem to be enough. A newspaper devoted to tropical rainforests and related themes was created that took the students to the next level of involvement. The students named their publication the *Tropical Tribune*. In the 1995–1996 school year, over 3,000 copies of the two issues were distributed to people in all 50 states and to 13 countries.

The *Tropical Tribune* is the only student-written newspaper in the country published for students, classes, and teachers regarding tropical rainforests. The newspaper provides accurate and reliable information about rainforests, the plight rainforests face, constructive conservation efforts, and ways to network student and teacher projects and interests. Readers of the *Tropical Tribune* have become more aware of circumstances surrounding rainforests. Many teachers and students use the *Tropical Tribune* to do class projects, to buy acres of rainforests, and to involve others in their school and community.

Reprinted with permission: Butch Beedle, J.C. McKenna Middle School

FIGURE 4.2 J.C. MCKENNA INTERDISCIPLINARY MODEL

Theme/Concept: ______________________________

Goals/Objectives: ______________________________

____

____

____

____

____

____

The Bait: ______________________________

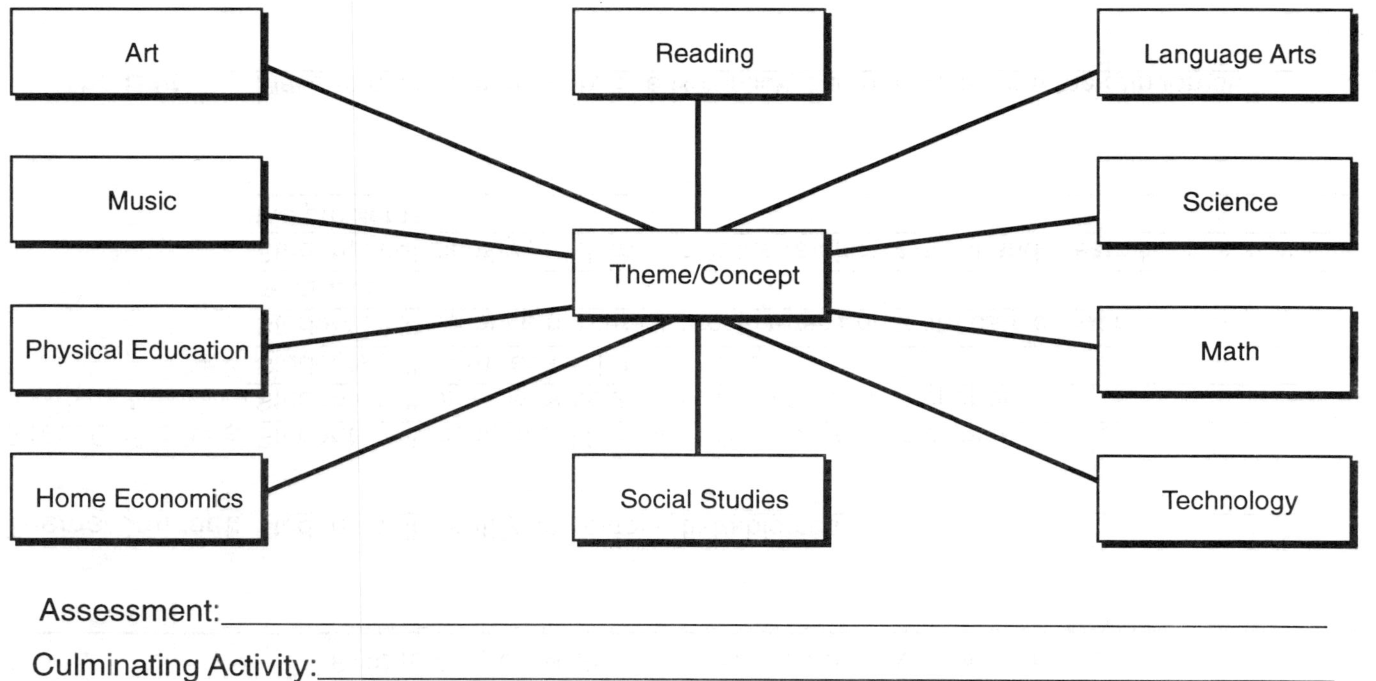
Art
Reading
Language Arts
Music
Science
Theme/Concept
Physical Education
Math
Home Economics
Social Studies
Technology
Assessment:
Culminating Activity:

FIGURE 4.3 J.C. MCKENNA INTERDISCIPLINARY MODEL

Theme/Concept: Students will identify and differentiate biomes.

Goals/Objectives: Students will recognize different writing styles in newspaper.
Students will write/produce a tropical rainforest newspaper.
Students will learn research techniques.
Students will describe rainforest ecosystems and learn causes for rainforest destruction.
Students will identify problems when the rainforest is cut and create solutions for the problems

The Bait: Make rainsticks, hear story The Rainstick, sample foods from the rain forest.

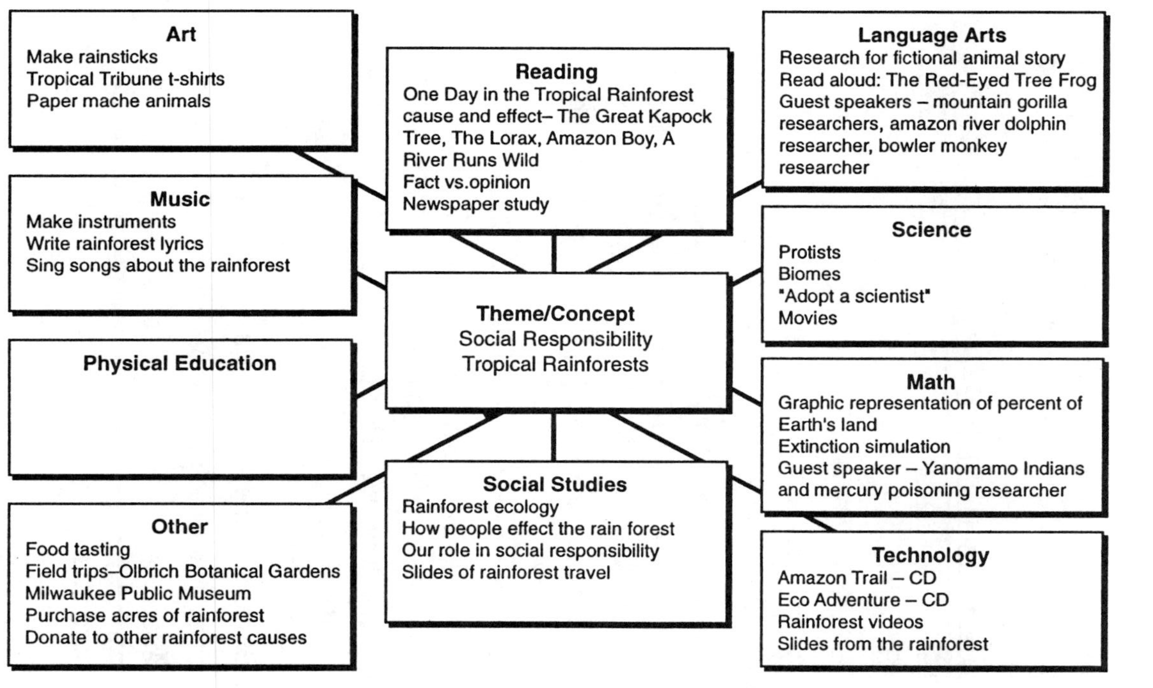

Assessment : Traditional exams, letter to the editor, biomes project, small group discussion, Tropical Tribune newspaper.

Culminating Activity: Tropical Tribune newspaper sharing.

FIGURE 4.4 DEVELOPMENT OF THE *TROPICAL TRIBUNE*

I. Students keep a log of potential stories from their class presentations, discussions, movies, slides, and speakers.

II. Students are divided into 4 groups at the end of the unit.

  A. Editorial

  B. Entertainment and Art

  C. News Stories

  D. Feature Stories

III. Groups brainstorm story ideas and assign topics.

IV. An entire day is blocked to begin the production of the newspaper.

  A. One classroom is set aside and staffed with all the resources necessary.

  B. Students conduct telephone interviews.

    1. Interviews include scientist, authors, environmentalists, film makers, and manufacturers.

    2. All interviews are taped.

  C. Students use research skills to find materials and take notes.

  D. Students write a rough draft of their story.

  E. Peer editors edit the story.

  F. After peer editing and teacher permission, students type their stories on the computer, making sure to save their work.

V. Student editors are chosen to help with decision-making, editing, and layout.

VI. A deadline is given for all stories to be completed.

VII. Teachers read stories and assist students with structure. Students are given individual guidance with their stories in order to create their best possible work.

VIII. All stories are printed on a laser copier with enamel paper.

IX. Student editors cut out stories. They begin to make choices about layout, quality and design for the newspaper.

X. The editors wax and manually lay out the paper on large sheets.

XI. The finished layout sheets are taken to the local newspaper. They then scan the photographs and print the newspaper.

XII. Nearly 3,000 newspapers are sent by bulk mail. The students do all the bundling and addressing to prepare for mailing.

XIII. The process begins again.

Reprinted with Permission:
6th Grade Staff, J.C. McKenna Middle School 1997

FIGURE 4.5 SAMPLE *TROPICAL TRIBUNE*

Spring 1997

Volume 4, Issue 2 J.C. McKENNA MIDDLE SCHOOL, EVANSVILLE, WISCONSIN

Our goal is to still bring you the best quality newspaper about the rain forest that we can. In preparation we had speakers about the Yanomamo Indians and pink river dolphins. We continue collecting current data on the topics we write. many devoted people and organizations continue to give us support financially and with their expertise. We appreciate all of this. We have exceeded our expectations and the demands of our paper are becoming overwhelming. Next year we will only produce one paper to reduce the time demands. Please continue to send us stories and ideas. Thanks again for all the encouragement. It makes the efforts worthwhile. The sixth grade students and staff at J. C. McKenna.

NEIL RETTIG
National Geographic Film maker
By Gina Kaiser and Rose Shumway

Neil Rettig is one of the top nature filmmakers in the world. His nature films have won 2 Emmys and numerous other awards. Neil films mostly for National Geographic, Nature and has done two I-Max films (this is a screen that is at least 3 stories tall).

One time Mr. Rettig was filming harpy eagles and an eagle attacked a sloth at 50 mph. In 2000 hours of sitting in blinds waiting to film, this is the only attack he has ever seen. Another time he fell out of a tree 60 feet in the air while climbing down from filming a baby harpy eagle hatching. Rettig ended up severely damaging his back.

Mr. Rettig started a reserve for harpy eagles in Guyana. The reserve was designed to prevent the harpy eagles from

Neil Rettig was 14 years old when he became interested in filmmaking. The first camera he used belonged to his parents. Neil's big dream was the harpy eagle. He has filmed eagles for 26 years. His speciality is filming harpy eagles.

Harpy eagles are one of the largest and most powerful eagles in the world. They are much larger and more powerful than a bald eagle. They can weigh up to 18 pounds. They can carry away sloths and monkeys that weigh up to 7 pounds. They eat 25 different kinds of tree living mammals. Unlike other eagles the harpy eagle does not soar, it stalks its prey from the branches of the upper canopy.

He enjoys filming harpy eagles in the Guyana rain forest. This interest includes many challenges for Rettig and this he likes. He found out from experience that birds of prey were very interesting. When filming he must wear a bullet proof vest and a helmet so he doesn't get attacked by a harpy eagle.

Filming harpy eagles is very difficult because their nests are 100 to 150 feet above the floor. The last time he filmed it took three years to find 8 nests that he could film. First, they have to climb up a tree to the nesting site. Then they build a platform like a tree fort to hide the camera. They build the blind slowly so not to scare the birds. Then they gradually begin filming. They spend at least 1000 hours sitting in the blind waiting for something to film. The baby eagle gives signals that the mother is coming. If you miss the chance to film, the mother may not return for another 2 to 3 days.

disappearing. This happens because of logging and people shooting and eating the eagles. The reserve is still in the planning stages. It will be in the Kanuku Mountains.

Mr. Rettig's hobby is falcon flying. Mr. Rettig has a falcon in which he flies outdoors in Wisconsin. He enjoys flying and caring for his pet.

Not too long ago Mr. Rettig went to the Arctic. He was filming the wildlife. There will be a National Geographic film out on NBC May 15, 1996 called Arctic Kingdom: Life on the Edge. The film won an award for his filmmaking. This trip took 2 years to film but you are only seeing 1 hour of it. Mr. Rettig warns not to get the wrong impression. The Arctic trip, Mr. Rettig says, has changed his life in miraculous ways.

If you want to see Mr. Rettig's pictures and story about harpy eagles look in February 1995 National Geographic.

Pentadiplandra Brazzeana (Sweet Stuff).......2
Jungle Medicines in Thailand........................4
Giant Worms..5
Entertainment..6 and 7
Jack Hanna's African Adventure....................8
Meet Robearto (a Bear on the Move)............10
Editorial...11 and 12
Where to Buy Acres of Rain Forest................13
Bugs as Snacks..14
Indian Troubles..15
V.O.I.C.E.S (Helping Ecuadorian Indians)....16

STREAMS: Science Teams in Rural Environments for Aquatic Management Studies

Grades 5–8

STREAMS is an interdisciplinary environmental curriculum developed for rural middle school students, which is intended to raise awareness and interest in water resources. As students learn more about water-related issues, they also discover that they can make a difference in solving water problems in the community. The curricular and instructional materials which have been developed for STREAMS are intended to be interdisciplinary in nature, and can be used in Social Studies, Science, Math, and Language Arts classes. Although individual teachers will find the program useful, the potential of the program is maximized when implemented by an interdisciplinary team of teachers.

STREAMS covers a wide variety of environmental and related topics, including acid rain, air pollution, groundwater, mathematical applications, outdoor education, pollution, recycling, the scientific method, statistics, technology, and wetlands. Examples of specific lessons are Erosion and Sedimentation, Household Pollutants, Nutrient Enrichment, and Stormwater Runoff. Students are involved in a range of activities when participating in these lessons, including experiments, field trips, problem solving, cooperative and discovery learning, hands-on learning, and independent study. It is important to note that in order to replicate this curriculum, teachers must have access to an outdoor environment *and* to a local stream.

The program was implemented in 1991 by Frederic Wilson and Timothy Julian, with funding provided by the Pennsylvania Bay Education Office, local businesses and industry, and private contributions. STREAMS has received recognition from several educational institutions, among them the Mid-Atlantic Regional Consortium for Mathematics and Science Education, Research for Better Schools: 1994 Promising Practice, and from Prentice-Hall / National Middle Schools Association: Grand Prize Team Teaching Award, 1996.

This program at Huntingdon Area Middle School involves an interdisciplinary team of four teachers — Social Studies, Science, Math, and Language Arts— with all teachers taking part in outdoor activities and field studies. All students participate in the core program, which involves 40 hours of time at the beginning of the school year dedicated to academic studies. After completion of the core, students may participate in environmental activities on a voluntary basis for the remainder of the year.

A SAMPLING OF ACTIVITIES

Students at Huntingdon Area Middle School are fortunate to be located near a small, but easily accessible watershed which is the site of STREAMS field activities. Among other activities, students tour the various housing developments within the 2.4 square mile Muddy Run Watershed to document positive and negative land management practices related to stormwater runoff, pollutants, sedimentation problems, and erosion. Water monitoring is done as well to determine the water quality of the watershed.

In addition to studying the Muddy Run Watershed, students also study the Stone Creek watershed from headwater to mouth to develop an awareness of the characteristics of a drainage basin. They determine the stream's depth, width, speed, volume, and temperature at four sites to document water quality, with particular attention given to nutrient enrichment.

The following is a summary of student involvement in a community service project that occurred as a result of participation in STREAMS.

FIGURE 4.6 REPLACING THE HOLLAND AVENUE SEWER LINE

Replacing the Holland Avenue Sewer Line

This was a on-going project involving students wanting to help this community resolve the environmental problems associated with the infiltration of groundwater into the Holland Avenue Sewage Line, and broken sewer lines in Huntingdon, Pennsylvania.

During field studies of the Muddy Run Watershed (1992 school year), students discovered an excessive amount of algae bloom in the stream. After conducting water quality monitoring tests and studying the situation further, students concluded that an enormous nutrient enrichment problem existed. Students alerted local and state authorities that a severe water pollution problem existed in the community. Initially, it was discovered that raw sewage was being discharged into the stream from specific sources. Immediate efforts were made by the borough to correct the identified sources of raw sewage, and the stream did show signs of improved water quality downstream.

As students continued to monitor the stream, conduct further water quality monitoring tests, and research more, they learned that the problem involved infiltration and overloading of the Holland Avenue Sewage Line with groundwater, stormwater runoff problems, and the sediment and erosion build-up in Muddy Run. They studied and researched solutions to correct the problem. They concluded that the best way to resolve the biggest percent of the problem (and the most expensive) was to replace the sewage pipelines.

Scores of letters were written during the 1993 school year to local and state officials asking them to act in resolving the problem. Then, during the 1993/94 school years the students organized a massive letter writing and petition drive. In March of 1994, students sent more well-documented letters and a petition with 595 middle and high school signatures to state officials requesting assistance in resolving the problem by fixing and/or replacing the broken sewage line.

These students convinced Pennsylvania officials of the town's need for a new sewage line. Officials at the Department of Environmental Resources were not only impressed with the students taking action, but also with the environmental knowledge they showed in their letters. The Center for Rural Pennsylvania and Research for Better Schools, Inc., both acknowledged the students' efforts in their respective newsletters, *Rural Notes* and *Currents*.

Activities such as these lead to an understanding of problems or practices which might negatively affect a watershed, as well as an understanding of how local water resources are interrelated to those of the larger Chesapeake Bay environment. Students are then able to generate solutions, in an attempt to solve water-related problems.

AN ADMINISTRATOR'S PERSPECTIVE

Jill Adams has been the principal at Huntingdon Area Middle School since the beginning of the STREAMS project, and is an enthusiastic supporter of the program. She believes that the STREAMS curriculum has been beneficial not only in terms of academic learning and community involvement, but has helped the school in reaching the goals of the district mission statement. Specifically, the program has promoted lifelong learning in both students and adults, as they become academically and emotionally involved in water resource issues and other environmental concerns of their community. Adams has also been impressed with the creativity and concern that come from involvement in STREAMS.

An unexpected outcome of the STREAMS program is an awareness that both students and teachers have gained in terms of the political ramifications of community action. For example, when students found evidence of waste in the water supply, they believed that everyone in the community would be as concerned and motivated to resolve the problem as they were. It came as something of a surprise, Adams notes, that there were those who were somewhat reluctant to take necessary action to clear up the waste problem. In another case, when students established a wetlands area in their community, they encountered concern from one neighbor who suspected that the wetlands was the cause of flooding in her yard. Initially, the students were disappointed that someone was not fully behind the wetlands plan; however, they decided to investigate the problem, and ended up educating the woman as to the real reason behind her flooding problem. This experience was rewarding in part because, Adams believes, it allowed the students to see that not only are they on the *learning* end of education, but they can also be on the *teaching* end, as they use their expertise to educate others.

SUCCESSES AND CHALLENGES

The involvement of students in voluntary activities has been very impressive, with a rate of participation of 60-75 percent. Students believe that they are learning something important, and that they are contributing to the greater community. They like the hands-on nature of the STREAMS curriculum, and teachers have seen a definite increase in student motivation and self-reliance.

- Discipline problems have been reduced significantly in the classes that participate in STREAMS. Post test unit scores taken from spring testing show that students retain what they have learned better than they do with a traditional curriculum.
- The STREAMS curriculum is able to accommodate different learning styles.
- Classroom study, field work, community service, and student collaboration give all students the chance to excel at what they do best.

- The benefits of the program for students go beyond the academic: community leaders have come to see Huntingdon students as effective partners in solving water related problems, and therefore have been more and more willing to provide financial support and other resources necessary for continuation of the program.

While students, teachers, administration, and the community all agree that STREAMS is overwhelmingly successful, there have nevertheless been challenges. Time for planning and monitoring the program has been insufficient, a challenge experienced by interdisciplinary teams across the country. Scheduling has also been an issue in implementing a program such as STREAMS. When the project was first started, there was a schoolwide free period (study hall) which was a time when all teachers and students could participate in STREAMS activities if they so chose. The free period has since been lost, so that it is now more difficult to coordinate STREAMS activities and projects.

Lack of money has also been a problem. As more and more students chose to participate in voluntary STREAMS activities, it became apparent that more money was needed to purchase equipment and supplies. Grants and community support have helped in this regard, but there is always a need for additional funds.

SUMMARY

The STREAMS project has been successful not only in terms of the cooperation it has generated between school and community, but also because of the enthusiasm of the students. They have been excited about environmental studies, and have put countless hours into identifying and solving water-related problems in the community. Their enthusiasm has, in fact, gone beyond the school environment, and has influenced community leaders as well.

Reprinted are several pages from the STREAMS project which may be of interest.

Contact: Project Director Frederic Wilson
Huntingdon Area Middle School
Huntingdon, Pennsylvania
814-643-2900

FIGURE 4.7 MACROINVERTEBRATE STUDY

Macroinvertebrate Study

Objectives of Macroinvertebrate Study:

- Use microscopes and stereoscopes to identify aquatic organisms
- Maintain the care of an Eco-Chamber
- Go out to the wetland between 11:19 and 12:00 to collect samples of plant and water life
- Identify organism collected from the wetlands
- Seek the knowledge of others through consultations with advanced biology students of Huntingdon Area High School
- Share our knowledge gained with others
- Learn to keep a scientific log and analyze our work
- Work in partnership with other sixth grade students in completing an independent study of our choice

Objectives of the Macroinvertebrate Study done by Huntingdon Area Middle School students. Reprinted with permission: Frederic Wilson. 1997.

FIGURE 4.8 RESEARCH HYPOTHESIS

Date: **January 8 through February 18, 1997**
Time: **11:19 AM - 12:08 PM**
Location: **Mr. Wilson's room (22)**
Intake/outflow of wetland adjacent to school

Contact People: Mr. Wilson, with the assistance of Miranda Crotsley and Heather Galbraith, advanced biology students at Huntingdon Area High School

Research Hypothesis: Before the actual project started, we thought that most of the organisms found would be in the Taxa Two and /or Taxa Three groups, even though our classes had found some Taxa One and Taxa Two organisms in the main channel of Muddy Run in September 1996. We thought this because the wetland is still in its early stage of development—constructed in August of 1996. Also, we were aware that the Holland Avenue Sewer Line had been replaced in the Summer and Fall of 1995. Previous water quality monitoring tests, 1991–1995, had shown Taxa Two and Three aquatic insects (predominantly Taxa Three). We believed that more Taxa One and Taxa Two organisms will live in the wetland as the plants purified the water, creating a habitat for organisms that cannot tolerate much pollution. This will happen because the area was once a natural wetland region.

Problem to Resolve: Identify macroinvertebrate aquatic organisms that live in the newly constructed HAMS wetland.

The hypothesis was written by students who conducted the Macroinvertebrate Study for STREAMS at Huntingdon Area Middle School. Reprinted with permission: Frederic Wilson, 1997.

FIGURE 4.9 SAMPLE *ENVIRONMENTAL TIMES*

The Environmental Times

Volume 1 Issue 1 January 1997

HAMS Students Receive Two Honors

By
Froggy Franny
&
Betty Butterfly

The students of the Huntingdon Area Middle School Environmental Club have received a citation from the Commonwealth of Pennsylvania, House of Representatives and a Borough Resolution for their many environmental projects and activities to benefit our community.

According to the citation, "The students have established environmental partnerships with community authorities to improve the living conditions of the Borough and have been positive representatives for their community across the commonwealth."

borough and have been positive representatives for their community across the Commonwealth; and

Whereas, The recipients of local, state and national awards, the students have brought great credit to themselves, their school and their community.

Now therefore, the House of Representatives of the Commonwealth of Pennsylvania congratulates the students from the Huntingdon Area Middle School upon their outstanding achievements in the STREAMS Environmental Program; heartily commend them for the exemplary citizenship which they have manifested, keeping with the highest ideals and values of this Commonwealth;

Rep. Larry O. Sather sponsored this citation for the students. The Citation and Resolution follow:

Commonwealth of Pennsylvania
The House of Representatives

Citation

Whereas, Students from Huntingdon Area Middle school are being recognized for their achievements in STREAMS Environmental Program, an environmental education and water study program supported by The Center for Rural Pennsylvania; and

Whereas, A model partnership between school and community, the program has brought together to work on numerous community environmental activities that have benefited the Borough of Huntingdon in the last six years; and

Whereas, The students have established environmental partnerships with community authorities to improve living conditions of the

And Directs that a copy of this citation, sponsored by the Honorable Larry O. Sather on October 4, 1996, be transmitted to Huntingdon Area Middle School, 2500 Cassady Avenue, Huntingdon, Pennsylvania 16652

Borough of Huntingdon
1001 Moore Street
Huntingdon PA 16652

RESOLUTION No. 13

RESOLUTION OF APPRECIATION HUNTINGDON ENVIRONMENTAL CLUB STUDENTS

WHEREAS, the Huntingdon Environmental Club Students have been engaged in numerous community environmental projects and activities, and

WHEREAS, these students have educated the community about the issue of storm water run-off, and

Journeys of Discovery: The Expeditions of Lewis and Clark and Zebulon Pike

Grades 5–8

The authors of The Expeditions of Lewis and Clark and Zebulon Pike and other Journeys of Discovery curriculum sourcebooks wrote these materials on the basic assumption that students and teachers are themselves explorers, and want to search for ideas and insights. To this end, the Journeys of Discovery lessons are organized around authentic daily entries from journals, letters, and other primary source materials from individuals such as Lewis and Clark, Zebulon Pike, Marco Polo, and others whose lives and times represent significant elements of our diverse cultural heritage. In this case, the curriculum is developed around the journals of Lewis and Clark, whose expedition was one of the most significant episodes in the history of the United States. In 1804–06, the Expedition carried not only the flag, but also the destiny of the young nation westward across thousands of miles of unknown land to the Pacific Ocean. Although they did not discover a Northwest Passage or a predictable transcontinental channel of commerce, their accomplishments were still formidable, influencing geopolitics, westward expansion, and scientific knowledge.

The Journeys approach is based on the idea that the best learner is a self-directed learner, capable of taking on and completing intellectually stimulating tasks as evidenced in the lives of great explorers, who were themselves writers and scientists, ethnographers and historians. To accomplish this, students are led through the readings to identify activities, topics, and resources that meet their needs at deeper levels of inquiry and enable them to make wide-ranging connections between the source material and the world today. It is believed that when students read primary source material, an intellectual transformation takes place. Primary sources, whether from Herodotus or Lewis and Clark, offer no conclusions and no "insights," thus opening new possibilities for creative thought.

Another idea central to the Journeys of Discovery approach is that of concrete activities associated with the daily readings. When hands-on activities are connected to readings, an intellectual renaissance becomes possible. The activities, whether drama, reports, construction, or experiments, are the basis of intellectual engagement. As writing is among the most important expressions of thought for purposes of evaluation, students are encouraged to follow the examples of great discoverers by journalizing throughout the year. Through literary experiences of their own design, learners can develop writing skills as they compile a unique portfolio of observations and discoveries along their own learning journey.

LESSON FORMAT

Lessons are generally organized in clusters of five to correspond to the regular school week, and each lesson consists of three parts. First, a study guide introduces each lesson with questions, project ideas, and information, providing a basis for more fully understanding the reading and highlighting the selection's significance. The second component of a lesson is the reading, an account that has been taken from original journals, letters, and the like. These readings have been organized to preserve the true expedition chronology. The third element of each lesson, besides the study guide and the reading, is an additional instructional resource in the form of a map, period literature selection, or other resource such as Native American tribal culture, history, and oral literature. Taken together, these lessons integrate reading, language, math, social studies, science, and the arts around the theme of discovery.

Examples of the Journeys of Discovery curriculum follow.

Contact:
Richard Scheuerman (509-648-3336) or
Arthur Ellis (206-281-2362)

FIGURE 4.10 FROM THOMAS JEFFERSON'S AUTOBIOGRAPHY

1. *My Great Good Fortune*

—from Thomas Jefferson's Autobiography

The tradition in my father's family was that their ancestor came to this country from Wales, and from near the mountain of Snowdown, the highest in Great Britain. I noted once a case from Wales, in the law reports, where a person of our name was either plaintiff or defendant; and one of the same name was secretary to the Virginia Company. These are the only instances in which I have met with the name in that country. I have found it in our early records; but the first particular information I have of any ancestor was of my grandfather, who lived at the place in Chesterfield called Ozborne's, and owned the lands afterwards the glebe of the parish. He had three sons; Thomas who died young, Field who settled on the waters of Roanoke and left numerous descendants, and Peter, my father, who settled on the lands I still own, called Shadwell, adjoining my present residence. He was born February 29, 1707-8, and intermarried 1739, with Jane Randolph, of the age of 19, daughter of Isham Randolph, one of the seven sons of that name and family, settled at Dungeness in Goochland. They trace their pedigree far back in England and Scotland, to which let everyone ascribe the faith and merit he chooses.

Wales *is one of four European countries that, together with England, Scotland, and Northern Ireland, make up the United Kingdom of Great Britain and Northern Ireland.*

The Virginia Company *was organized in 1606 by a group of London businessmen as the first joint stock company for the development of lands in Virginia. Captain John Smith was a leader of the company's colony established at Jamestown in 1607.*

The glebe *was a parcel of land given to a pastor in*

recognition of his service to a parish.

A pedigree *is one's lineage, or line of ancestors.*

My father's education had been quite neglected; but being of a strong mind, sound judgment, and eager after information, he read much and improved himself, insomuch that he was chosen, with Joshua Fry, Professor of Mathematics in William and Mary College, to continue the boundary line between Virginia and North Carolina, which had been begun by Colonel Byrd; and was afterwards employed with the same Mr. Fry, to make the first map of Virginia which had ever been made, that of Captain Smith being merely a conjectural sketch. They possessed excellent materials for so much of the country as is below the Blue Ridge; little being then known beyond that ridge. He was the third or fourth settler, about the year 1737, of the part of the country in which I live. He died, August 17th, 1757, leaving my mother

"On the lands I still own"

FIGURE 4.10 FROM THOMAS JEFFERSON'S AUTOBIOGRAPHY, CONTINUED

a widow, who lived till 1776, with six daughters and two sons, myself the elder. To my younger brother he left his estate on James River, called Snowden, after the supposed birth-place of the family: to myself, the lands on which I was born and live.

He placed me at the English school at five years of age; and at the Latin at nine, where I continued until his death. My teacher, Mr. Douglas, a clergyman from Scotland, with the rudiments of the Latin and Greek languages, taught me the French; and on the death of my father, I went to the Reverend Mr. Maury, a correct classical scholar, with whom I continued two years; and then, to sit, in the spring of 1760, went to William and Mary College, where I continued two years. It was my great good fortune, and what probably fixed the destinies of my life, that Dr. William Small of Scotland, was then professor of Mathematics, a man profound in most of the useful branches of science, with a happy talent of communication, correct and gentlemanly manners, and an enlarged and liberal mind.

Fortunately, the philosophical chair became vacant soon after my arrival at college, and he was appointed to fill it per interim: and he was the first who ever gave, in that college, regular lectures in Ethics, Rhetoric and

Latin and Greek *are languages that were often studied by students in Jefferson's time in order to better understand the important ideas of these ancient peoples, the Bible, and to foster an appreciation for the order of their grammar and quality of expression. Latin was the language of the ancient Romans which spread over Western Europe and developed into "Romance" languages like French, Spanish, and Italian.*

Belles Lettres. He returned to Europe in 1762, having previously filled up the measure of his goodness to me, by procuring for me, from his most intimate friend, George Wythe, a reception as a student of law, under his direction, and introduced me to the acquaintance and familiar table of Governor Fauquier, the ablest man who had ever filled that office. With him, and at his table, Dr. Small and Mr. Wythe, his amici omnium horarum, and myself, formed a partie quartee, and to the habitual conversations on these occasions I owed much instruction. Mr. Wythe continued to be my faithful and beloved mentor in youth, and my most affectionate friend through life. In 1767, he led me into the practice of the law at the bar of the General court, at which I continued until the Revolution.

William and Mary College *is the second oldest institution of higher learning in America. It is located in Williamsburg, Virginia and was founded in 1693 by King William III and Queen Mary II of England.*

belles lettres *(bellet)*: *From the French words belles (beautiful) and lettres which refer to works of literature highly regarded for their style and meaning.*

amici ommium horarum: *Latin for "a friend of all hours."*

partie quartee: *Latin for "a group of four."*

FIGURE 4.11 DISCUSSION GUIDE

Directions: Please check each statement which you can support and be prepared to cite your evidence from your reading and experience.

Definitions and Knowledge:

_____ 1. Thomas Jefferson grew up in Virginia.

_____ 2. Jefferson's father was a self-educated man who learned by reading.

_____ 3. Jefferson's father was employed by a college professor to set the boundary line between Virginia and North Carolina.

_____ 4. Jefferson's father valued his liberal education at William and Mary College.

_____ 5. Jefferson's father died before Thomas went to College.

_____ 6. Jefferson highly valued his liberal education at William and Mary College.

_____ 7. A professor of math from Scotland greatly influenced Jefferson's thinking.

Comprehension–apply knowledge to experiences and concepts:

_____ 1. Jefferson's family came from England and Scotland.

_____ 2. During Jefferson's boyhood, southern Virginia was uncharted, frontier wilderness.

_____ 3. Jefferson assumed early responsibility within his family.

_____ 4. Jefferson learned more than math from Scottish professor William Small.

_____ 5. Jefferson ultimately became a lawyer.

Evaluation–judgments about the value of ideas, objects and actions:

_____ 1. Education makes a people easy to lead but difficult to drive; easy to govern; but impossible to enslave. Lord Brougham

_____ 2. The things taught in schools and colleges are not an education, but the means of education. Emerson

_____ 3. A liberal mind is an open mind.

_____ 4. A liberal arts education broadens one's mind but is useless for vocation.

Colonial Times and the Revolutionary War

Eighth Grade

The eighth grade teachers at Bartlett Middle School in Lowell, Massachusetts, had been teaching interdisciplinary units for several years when Steven Cyr and Mark Souza developed an experimental, hands-on interdisciplinary unit during the summer of 1996. While there had been general acceptance of interdisciplinary studies that involved "traditional" assignments such as worksheets, the new approach was met with much skepticism, in large part because it was seen as being too "elementary" in nature. The new unit was designed for eighth grade students and integrated all curricular subjects. "This stuff is all right for younger kids, but this is eighth grade!" was but one of the comments heard by Cyr and Souza. They persevered, however, and won over many of the skeptics.

This interdisciplinary curriculum is actually two units that cover Colonial Times and the Revolution. Working together during summer vacation, Cyr and Sousa worked with a third teacher to develop a curriculum for eighth graders based on a similar, successful project piloted a year earlier with sixth graders. Teachers in the district had been trained in the EDC method of curriculum development for two summers, which was helpful, according to Cyr, in developing these interdisciplinary units. Beginning with desired outcomes, the units integrated social studies, language, reading, the arts, and math. While it received a lukewarm response from teachers, administrators were enthusiastic about the venture, particularly after the initial success with sixth graders. Student response was unequivocally positive as well, judging from comments made to teachers and parents, and from responses made on evaluations.

A SAMPLING OF ACTIVITIES

Teachers began implementation of the new curriculum during the second week of school with field trips to various historical sites around the Salem area. These were followed by a project designed to acquaint students with the countries that initially settled and colonized America. On a map of Europe, students were asked to choose three countries that colonized America, and then do research to find out which routes they traveled to reach their destinations in North America where colonies were established. In addition, students wrote letters "home," describing the journey to the new world as if they were actually experiencing it.

Following the colonization project, students made "Colonial Encyclopedias," books that included entries that describe life in America with accompanying illustrations. In music class, students learned songs and instruments of the Colonial and Revolutionary periods, while in art they made the backdrop and costumes for a period play.

Research and presentation skills were put to the test when students worked in cooperative groups of 4–5 to investigate one of the major battles of the Revolutionary War. After about two weeks, each group was given one class period to teach their battle to the rest of the class, including who did the fighting, where the battle occurred, action, and the outcome of the battle. The presentation involved preparation of a study guide for class members, a worksheet and test related to the battle, and a visual representation. A rubric outlined expectations for the presentation.

The curriculum culminated with an exhibition at the end of January, which involved all eighth grade teachers and students. Each teacher identified a different aspect of colonial life after which the students designed a booth to share their piece of early America with the rest of the school (See Figure 1.) One group of students, for example, learned tinsmithing, which they taught to other students who came to visit their booth. Some students became "experts" at the art of stenciling, while others shared quilting, candle making, and foods of the period. A highlight of the exhibitions, according to Steven Cyr, was the play presented by one of the lower level reading groups. These students perfected and performed an original seven-minute play depicting the ratification of the Declaration of Independence. Their abilities were inspiring and impressive, both to the audience and to class members themselves.

SUCCESSES AND CHALLENGES

Successes that resulted from this interdisciplinary curriculum included:

- A high level of involvement and excitement on the part of students, teachers, and administrators
- Increased self-confidence in presentation abilities by students
- An understanding of colonial life and the Revolutionary War from a wide range of cultural and political perspectives
- A sense of accomplishment and achievement demonstrated in the final exhibition
- Support for interdisciplinary studies by teachers initially reluctant to the idea.

The following frustrations were noted by Cyr and Sousa:

- Length of the unit — both developers agreed that time spent on the curriculum could be shortened
- Initial reluctance by other teachers to interdisciplinary studies
- Student performance on more traditional assessments was somewhat disappointing

While Cyr and Sousa plan to teach their Colonial Times / Revolutionary War curriculum again next year, they plan some refinements and adjustments. They will, for example, shorten the total time spent on these two particular units, but continue the interdisciplinary approach with studies of the Constitution and the Civil War.

Contact:
Steven Cyr, Mark Souza
Bartlett Middle School, Lowell, MA
508-937-8968

FIGURE 4.13 COLONIAL CLOTHING

Colonial Clothing: From the interdisciplinary unit "Colonial Times and the Revolutionary War." Christina Lumenello, Bartlett Middle School. Reprinted with permission.

Clothing

Clothing was hand made in Colonial times. They had to spin the wool they got from sheep and flax they got from plants into cloth. Then all the cloth had to be hand sewn into garments. People wore wool in the winter time because it kept them warm. They wore linen in the summer time so they would stay cool.

Shoes, also, had to be made by hand. They were mostly made from leather, although some women's shoes were made from linen or silk. People who made leather for a living were called tanners. Leather was made from the hides of animals.

Women had many styles of shoes. From boots to flats to pumps. If you were wealthy you probably owned many pairs of shoes, but if you were of lower class you would have owned maybe only one pair of shoes. Ladies wore clogs and pattens to protect their shoes from the mud. Men sometimes wore clogs, too. Wealthy

FIGURE 4.13 COLONIAL CLOTHING, CONTINUED

men wore flat shoes on special occasions that looked like ladies shoes. They mostly wore leather boots.

Simple cotton and linen was worn by most Colonial women, but wealthy women wore beautiful, expensive, silk gowns. They also wore colorful bonnets and hats, and lacy gloves.

Men wore breeches, which are knee-length pants, instead of long pants. They wore loose fitting shirts with ruffles around the collar.

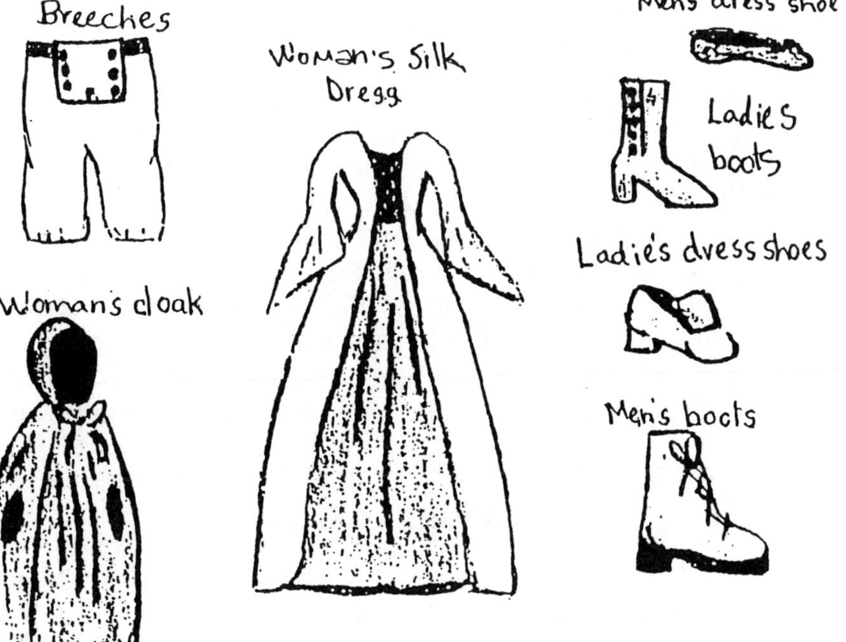

Integrated Teaching and Learning: History and English

Ninth Grade

On the drive home from a Coalition of Essential Schools forum in the spring of 1995, North Kansas City High School teachers Helen Bridges and Rhonda Franke discovered they shared a common interest in curriculum integration. They were, in fact, covering much of the same material in their respective English and history classes. Rather than continue their separate efforts, they decided to collaborate on the development of an interdisciplinary curriculum for their ninth grade English and history students. A proposal was made to the principal, who was very supportive of the plan and granted approval for implementation of the curriculum for the following school year.

Helen and Rhonda worked throughout the summer, spending 2–3 days a week in the development of an outline of the curriculum for the entire school year, as well as to identify projects and activities that would support the curriculum. While the outline served them well that first year, some revisions were made before moving ahead to the second year. Their success has prompted the administration to ask that all teachers of freshman students take an interdisciplinary approach to English and history.

A Sampling of Activities

Students start the year with a unit on Immigration, designed to develop an awareness of those culture groups that have settled in America. Working in cooperative groups, students research a particular culture group, with each student in the group being responsible for a specific part of a final presentation. They are expected to know and share with the class reasons why their culture group came to the United States, where they settled, how they developed or changed over the years, and the current status of the group. History, geography, poetry, and short stories are included in the unit. In addition, students research the music, clothing, and food embraced by their culture group, and incorporate these into the final presentation.

A second unit centers on the Depression years, where students again research various aspects of this period of history. To get a firsthand understanding of life during the 1920s and 1930s, students are expected to interview a person who experienced those years, and to include their findings as part of a final report. Helen and Rhonda noted that while the interview is a valuable part of the unit, both cognitively and emotionally, they have since revised the unit to include World War II so that students might have an easier time locating interviewees who can discuss the events and challenges of the period. *To Kill a Mockingbird* is one of the literature selections that students read as part of this unit, and guest speakers are invited to address the students on any number of topics related to the Depression and World War II.

SUCCESSES AND CHALLENGES

Helen and Rhonda are pleased with the success of their integrated curriculum, particularly with the response they have had from students. They see their students becoming excited about the curriculum and enthusiastically engaging in learning. In addition, they find that the students who are part of the integrated classes experience a sense of community which was not apparent in the traditional curriculum model. Further, Rhonda has tracked test scores and course grades for students in both her integrated classes and her traditional history classes, and notes that fewer of the integrated students fail the class.

They have faced several challenges in implementing an interdisciplinary curriculum, however. The most serious of these has been with the scheduling process; that is, having their integrated students assigned to the same schedule, so that each teacher has the same students for those classes. A second challenge has been the fact that they do not share a classroom. During the first year, they each had separate rooms at opposite ends of the school, and while they have since been assigned rooms closer to each other, they have not yet been able to occupy adjoining rooms. When they do get both classes together, it involves moving to the cafeteria or the gym, a workable but complicated solution. It has been difficult, therefore, to schedule lessons which are team-taught, or to have speakers come and address both classes of students together. While these issues may be frustrating, they are not insurmountable. The necessity of moving between classrooms, for example, requires a certain level of maturity and responsibility. For the most part, their students have demonstrated the ability to do this, thereby lessening the limitation inherent in separate classrooms.

A final point of consideration. Experience has shown Rhonda and Helen that personality is important when making the decision to collaborate for curriculum integration. That is, teachers who undertake this kind of curricular restructuring will spend a significant amount of time planning, assessing, and revising, and so should have a positive, supportive working relationship.

The following is a portion of the Immigration Unit outline developed by Helen and Rhonda, as well as the related assignments.

Contact:
Helen Bridges
Rhonda Franke
North Kansas City High School
North Kansas City, MO
816-221-0185

FIGURE 4.14 IMMIGRATION UNIT OUTLINE

II. IMMIGRATION
   A. Theme: Self-Identity
   B. History
      1. Immigration
      2. Impact of Immigration on Society
   C. Literature
      1. "Clothes Make the Man"
      2. "The Confrontation"
      3. "The Fight"
      4. "Why Don't You Wear Shoes?"
      5. "Best Foot Forward"
      6. "Number One Son"
      7. "Story of an Immigrant"
      8. Excerpt from "The Jungle- Immigrating from Lithuania," pp. 26-34
   D. Poetry
      1. "Thumbprint"
      2. "Grandma"
      3.. "John Doe, Jr."
   E. Composition
      1. Informative paragraph on immigration:

         In groups, students choose one group of immigrants to study upon entry to the U.S.
      2. Letter about being an immigrant

FIGURE 4.15 GROUP IMMIGRATION PROJECT

Group Immigration Project

Immigrants came to the United States from many different countries. The purpose of this project is to learn more about these ethnic groups that came to the United States during the late 1800s and into the twentieth century. Each group will be required to prepare a presentation and informative paragraph about an ethnic culture.

Your topic is ______________________________

Each group will be required to give a presentation and write an informative paragraph on one of the following aspects of this immigrant group. Each area must be covered and each person is responsible for at least one area. If there are two people in your group, omit the second area. If you would like to, you may do this part for extra credit. Before you begin researching, you must tell Mrs. Franke or Mrs. Bridges what area each group member has chosen and write it down.

<u>History/Old Culture:</u> Explain the history of this country, what it was like to live in this country in the past, problems that might have caused people to want to leave the country.

<u>Why Came/Where Settled:</u> Explain why these immigrants came to the U.S., in what part of the country they settled, and why they chose that area.

<u>Culture in U.S. and Contributions:</u> Explain what this immigrant group's culture is like, language used today, type of dress, religion, how they live in the U.S.. Explain what things this immigrant group has brought to the U.S., such as words, dress, food, and famous people.

Presentation

Each group member must present his/her own researched part of the project. You may only use a 3X5 notecard with an outline written on it. You may not read your paragraph

FIGURE 4.15 GROUP IMMIGRATION PROJECT, CONTINUED

word for word. In addition to presenting your information, you will also explain a visual aid that will help illustrate your part of the project. You will only be graded on your part of the presentation. This portion of the project will be worth 55 points.

Visual Aid

Each member must create a visual aid for his/her project. Listed below are some possible ideas for a visual aid. One group member may bring in food as a visual aid. This would be a good aid for the contributions or culture person. If you choose to bring food as a visual aid, you must bring enough to share with the class and be able to explain its relationship to your project. Each group is encouraged to work together on the visual aids; however, each person will only receive a grade for the aid that he/she explained during the presentation. You will be allowed to work on your visual aid in class if you need to. If you need paper for any type of visual aid, it can be supplied for you. Be creative!! This portion of the project will be worth 30 points.

timelines	posters	skit	murals	food
music	mobiles	video	costume/clothing	

Schedule

Monday October 14: Meet in Room 57 for 5th and 6th blocks. Both classes will be in the library 7th block. The group topics will be handed out and further instructions will be given. We will then be working in the library for the remainder of the class periods. Reminder: You will not be allowed to check out any books, so make sure that you use your time wisely in class. DUE AT END OF PERIOD: LIST OF GROUP RESPONSIBILITIES (5 points).

Tuesday/Wednesday, October 15/16: Meet in the library. We will be working in the library during this period. DUE

FIGURE 4.15 GROUP IMMIGRATION PROJECT, CONTINUED

AT END OF PERIOD: A LIST OF AT LEAST THREE SOURCES USED AND TEN FACTS ABOUT TOPIC (10 points).

Thursday/Friday, October 17/18: Go to your regular classes. We will be working in the classroom preparing visual aids and organizing the presentations. No one will be allowed to go to the library unless they were absent the previous day. DUE AT THE END OF THE PERIOD: A VISUAL AID OR PLAN FOR VISUAL AID AND PREPARED PRESENTATION (10 points).

Monday, Tuesday, and Wednesday: Group Presentations. Meet in Room 57 for 5th and 6th block. Meet in the Auditorium for 7th block. You must be ready to give your presentation on these dates. If you are absent the day of your presentation, you will be required to give your presentation on the following class period; the rest of the group must be ready to give the presentation without you! If you or your group is not prepared, half credit will be deducted from any presentation not ready.

Grades

Enclosed in your packet is a copy of the rubric explaining how you will be graded. You must keep this sheet and return it to Mrs. Franke before your presentation. Failure to do so will result in loss of points.

Group responsibilities	5 points
3 Sources and 10 Facts	10 points
Work on Thursday/Friday	5 points
Oral Presentation	55 points
Visual Aid	30 points

ABC'S OF INTERDISCIPLINARY PROJECTS

NINTH GRADE

At Parkview High School in Springfield, Missouri, Linda DeBusk has been developing and teaching a ninth grade interdisciplinary curriculum for the past five years. She and colleague LaReva Newcomer began their journey by collaborating on an integrated English / social studies block for their classes of low-achieving students. After two years, the project expanded to include a math and a science teacher. While the planning becomes somewhat more difficult with four teachers and four different subjects, the rewards for students seem to be worth the effort, DeBusk believes.

PLANNING FOR INTEGRATION OF THE CURRICULUM

Whether you are integrating two, three, or four subjects, DeBusk and her colleagues offer several suggestions to those who are moving in the direction of interdisciplinary studies. First of all, they have found that teachers should choose topics or themes that they themselves find interesting, challenging, and motivating—topics that "grab your interest," according to DeBusk. She describes as an example a unit she and Newcomer developed and taught on the Westward Movement—"Missouri Westward—which was based in part on the writings of Laura Ingalls Wilder. These books were favorites of the two teachers, but were—surprisingly—unfamiliar to many of their students. The readings inspired such activities as newspaper writing, journaling, cooking (apple butter), and map skills. Students were also taken on a field trip to the home of Laura Ingalls Wilder.

A second theme that was developed by the team of four centered on the centennial celebration of the St. Louis World's Fair and Olympics. The event was local, current, and exciting, and provided a wealth of opportunity for study in each of the subject areas: English, social studies, math, and science. The unit was implemented toward the end of the 1997 school year, and involved a trip to the site of the St. Louis Fair as well as a unit / year-end exhibition. Both of these units were interesting to the teachers, and their interest and enthusiasm were channeled into the curriculum, resulting in a timely, engrossing academic project for students.

In addition to choosing motivating themes for study, the teachers note the need for significant blocks of time for planning, both in the initial stages of developing the curriculum, and throughout the implementation stages. In the case of the Parkview teachers, a grant allowed them to buy release time to begin their planning. Five years later, the teachers' schedules give them a common plan time every other day, of which they use 30–45 minutes a week in curriculum collaboration. In addition, several meetings are typically held in the summer to set a general course for the school year.

Finally, the success of an integrated curriculum is at least somewhat dependent on students' schedules. DeBusk notes that her team of four teachers were frustrated in their first-year attempt to integrate the curriculum, not because of academic issues, but rather because of scheduling difficulties. The large number of "non-integrated" students in each of their four classes made it difficult to maintain any sense of continuity across classes or content cohesion. Thus, curriculum integration is necessarily influenced to some degree by the limitations inherent in scheduling. Administrative support is crucial in this regard, although even this cannot guarantee an absence of scheduling conflicts.

Contact:
Linda DeBusk
Parkview High School, Springfield, MO 65807
417 895-2775

HORIZON HIGH SCHOOL: A SCHOOL-WIDE MODEL OF INTERDISCIPLINARY TEACHING

GRADES 9–12

When Horizon High School opened in the Fall of 1988, it had as one of its goals the integration of curriculum. In the nine years since, the program at Horizon has grown from one that involved 500 students and grade-level, interdisciplinary courses, to one that now involves 1500 students, 20 teaching teams, and 3-period interdisciplinary core classes. A supportive administration and teachers committed to an interdisciplinary philosophy have ensured the growth and success of the integrated model at Horizon.

A BRIEF HISTORY

When the Horizon staff welcomed its first classes of sophomores and juniors in the Fall of 1988, they offered an interdisciplinary block of classes for sophomores which included one credit each of English/writing and American history, and a half credit each of science and art. With very few curricular materials and no library, they faced a challenging year. However, the teachers who came to Horizon had applied for teaching positions at the school up to a year before and were committed to the concept of interdisciplinary studies. Nevertheless, Diane Marino notes that being one of the few high schools in the country that was embracing an interdisciplinary approach at the time, they had few leads to follow and, therefore, operated to some extent by trial and error. For example, they found that offering half credits of science and art did not meet the needs of students, and eventually dropped art from the core and added science as a full credit course. The art coordinators did continue to work with core students, however. Besides the difficulty with art and science credits, classes were too large, with some having 145 students for three teachers. On the positive side, however, teachers found success in using a thematic approach to teaching the curriculum, and continue to use themes in the current model. In addition, the physical plant facilitated an interdisciplinary approach, with large, connecting rooms designed to accommodate combined classes. All in all, it turned out to be a disjointed year, but one from which they learned important lessons about the necessary elements of a successful integrated program.

At the request of students, core classes were added for juniors and seniors, including World History and World Literature. After experiencing integrated classes during tenth grade, the students wanted similar courses during their junior and senior years. While this World History and World Literature have served as the foundation of the upper level interdisciplinary program, there are other combinations of courses which are team taught, including sociology/psychology, business (law)/social studies, and algebra/geometry. A course in British literature and theater is being added, as well as an English/Social Studies course focused on the Great Books. This class is driven by philosophical issues and concepts.

In the fall of 1994, ninth graders began attending Horizon for the first time. The program designed for them, called SEGA, integrates Science, English, Geography, and Art, and was developed by tenth grade teachers already experienced in curriculum integration, as well as incoming ninth grade teachers. In addition to the core classes—social studies (economics and World History), English (World Literature and adolescent literature), and science (physical and earth science, astronomy, and meteorology)—students fill in their schedules with math, keyboarding, health/P.E., and music or art classes. Ninth grade students begin the year with an introductory unit aimed at teaching group process skills, study skills, seminar involvement, and other strategies deemed necessary for a successful high school experience. This is followed by four additional thematic units during the remainder of the year, the final project being a mock United Nations summit meeting. This culminating unit allows students to apply all their knowledge to a given topic. Specifically, students are asked to identify a world nation and research that nation with respect to a given "real life" problem (for example, unchecked migration). Students research their nation's resources, government, quality of life, physical systems, geography, and the like, to determine what impact the problem has on the people and land. Part of the project involves writing a position paper on the effects of the problem on their nation, as well as the effect it has on neighboring nations. The discussion is finally taken to an international level (the UN), where the global impact of the problem is discussed.

RECOMMENDATIONS

While the teachers at Horizon have experienced frustrations over the past nine years, their commitment to interdisciplinary studies has encouraged them to persevere , and in so doing they offer advice that might be useful to those just beginning the transition to integrated curriculum.

1. Time for planning is essential! Teachers experienced in interdisciplinary curriculum development stress the need for large blocks of planning time, not only in the beginning, but also when teams are changed or at the beginning and end of integrated units. Teachers at Horizon meet at the end of the school year to debrief, refine, and revise their units, and they meet anywhere from 60 minutes a day to 60 minutes a week during the school year for ongoing planning. Common plan time with team members is also a must.
2. Be prepared to struggle with scheduling. There is no way around this, it seems, and the more classes you attempt to integrate, the more challenging it becomes. Even with the support of the administration and the scheduling personnel, it is difficult to schedule integrated classes without impacting the elective choices. Patience and determination are critical!

3. One class or subject area must drive the curriculum. According to Diane, teachers at Horizon found that they could not develop an integrated curriculum around three classes or subjects; they needed to decide on one content area which will drive the curriculum, and have the other one or two serve to enrich and complement that one. For example, their ninth grade curriculum is driven by science and geography, while tenth grade has American History as its focus, eleventh grade centers on World History, and twelfth grade on philosophical issues and themes (essential questions).

Horizon's experience at designing and implementing a schoolwide integrated curriculum demonstrates that the process is one that takes time, and must evolve over the course of several years. But the benefits are worth the effort: students enjoy the interdisciplinary nature of learning, and begin to make connections between content areas that are typically taught and learned separately or in isolation. When the teaching staff and administration are committed to an interdisciplinary philosophy, as they have been at Horizon, the potential for long-term success is greatly increased.

Contact:
Kathy Coccetti
Linda Fiorella
Diane Marino
Horizon High School, Brighton, CO
303-450-5227

5

Interdisciplinary Curricular Resources

A Middle School Curriculum: From Rhetoric to Reality

2nd Edition. James A. Beane. National Middle School Association. Columbus, Ohio. 1993.

A World of Maps and Travel: An Interdisciplinary Curriculum and Resource Packet Designed for Secondary Students

A World of Maps and Travel: An Interdisciplinary Curriculum and Resource Packet Designed for Secondary Students looks to strengthen map skills and develop an awareness of the history of maps in high school students. The four units of study guide the student in the development of a map project, using new knowledge and skills, as well as computer technology. The curriculum was developed by Helen Sherman, and can be accessed through:

ERIC Document 369725.

Africa, Europe, and Asia: Ready-to-use Interdisciplinary Lessons & Activities for Grades 5–12 (Social Studies Curriculum Activities Library, Vol 2)

Dwila Bloom. Center for Applied Research in Education. 1997. ISBN 0876285906.

America: Ready-to-use Interdisciplinary Lessons & Activities for Grades 5–12 (Social Studies Curriculum Activities Library, Vol.1)

Dwila Bloom. Center for Applied Research in Education. 1997. ISBN 0876285892.

Attitudes of Science and Social Studies Teachers toward Interdisciplinary Instruction. Barman, C. & Rusch, J.J. (1982). *American Biology Teacher, 44*, 421–426

In the course of evaluating teachers' attitudes toward interdisciplinary curriculum, the authors recommend a program called SCATE (Students Concerned About tomorrow's Environment). This program was developed to encourage high school students to explore environmental problems, and to devise ways of acting to resolve those problems.

Bridging the Gap: Integrating Curriculum in Upper Elementary and Middle Schools

Cora Lee Five and Marie Dionisio. Heinemann. Portsmouth, NH. 1996.

Career Choices Curriculum

Published by Academic Innovations, this curriculum was designed to be used in English/Language Arts, Math, Social Studies, and/or School to Work classes. It is appropriate for 8th–10th grade students, and allows opportunities for these teens to undertake reading, writing, and computation assignments that illustrate the connection between school, success at work, and satisfaction in life. *Career Choices* integrates academics and guidance to give students greater understanding of themselves. Contact Academic Innovations for further information: http://www.academicinnovations.com.

CHALLENGING STUDENTS WITH THE LAW: AN INTERDISCIPLINARY CURRICULUM FOR GIFTED AND TALENTED STUDENTS AT THE UPPER ELEMENTARY AND MIDDLE SCHOOL LEVELS

Challenging Students with the Law: An Interdisciplinary Curriculum for Gifted and Talented Students at the Upper Elementary and Middle School Levels, was written by Julia Ann Gold and others, in conjunction with the University of Puget Sound, Tacoma, WA, and the Institute for Citizen Education and the Law, and was sponsored by the Department of Education, Washington D.C. This curriculum consists of eight units which cover the legal aspects of several controversial issues, including old growth forests, animal rights, freedom of speech, and the internment of Japanese Americans. Lessons integrate several content areas and encourage interactive, cooperative learning through case studies, role playing, and simulations. Activities are designed to incorporate Gardner's multiple intelligences.

ERIC Document 388536.

CITYWORKS

Cityworks is a multidisciplinary, project-based approach to the curriculum designed for students in grades 9–12. The program attempts to make connections between vocational education and academics, by creating links between the economic needs of the local community and vocational education. Projects encourage cooperative work, based on problem-posing, reflection, and problem solving. This program is based at Rindge School of Technical Arts in Cambridge, MA.

Contact: Larry Rosenstock, Executive Director (617) 349-6751.

COMMUNITY SOLUTIONS TO SOLID WASTE POLLUTION. OPERATION WASTE WATCH: THE THREE R'S FOR ELEMENTARY SCHOOL, GRADE 6

Community Solutions to Solid Waste Pollution. Operation Waste Watch: The Three R's for Elementary School, Grade 6 focuses on waste management issues. Students study the waste management system and problems in their own communities, and devise model waste management plans. Objectives relate primarily to science; however, the curriculum is interdisciplinary in nature and integrates social studies, health, language arts, mathematics, and art to some extent. The program was published by the Virginia State Department of Waste Management, and can be accessed through:

ERIC Document 347079.

CONNECTING PATTERNS THROUGH ENVIRONMENTAL EDUCATION. JOHNSON, P. (1983). *EDUCATIONAL LEADERSHIP*, *40*(7), 40–44

This article describes a class in which high school students studied the shores of Maine's northeast coast and published an oceanography newsletter discussing their findings. The class combined in-class studies with field study in preparation for producing the newsletter.

DESIGNING INTERDISCIPLINARY CURRICULUM IN MIDDLE, JUNIOR HIGH, AND HIGH SCHOOLS

Richard E. Maurer. Allyn and Bacon, Boston. 1994.

DESIGNING WITH RIGOR: CRAFTING INTERDISCIPLINARY HIGH SCHOOL CURRICULA

Heidi Hayes Jacobs. The High School Magazine, 4 (3). March/April, 1997. 32–39. This article discusses guidelines to consider when designing interdisciplinary curriculum projects, as well as templates for curriculum planning and helpful references.

DISCOVERING PATTERNS IN THE BUILT ENVIRONMENT

Discovering Patterns in the Built Environment is an interdisciplinary curriculum designed by the Center for Arts and Sciences in Oklahoma. Specifically intended for gifted and disadvantaged students, the curriculum is intended to help students understand the various styles of architecture, and to make connections to other areas. For a discussion of details of the curriculum, see:

Making Connections through Architecture. Patricia Hollingsworth (1993). *Gifted Child Today, 16,* (5), 6–8.

DISSOLVING BOUNDARIES: TOWARD INTEGRATIVE CURRICULUM

Edward N. Brazee and Jody Capelluti. National Middle School Association. Columbus, Ohio. 1995.

HUMANITAS

Humanitas is a grade 7–12 curriculum designed to help students approach the humanities through interdisciplinary units. The topics of these units include "Roots of Prejudice" and "Industrial Capitalism," among others. The units are structured to encourage students to make use of original sources in conducting research in order to understand abstract concepts. The project is funded primarily by the Los Angeles Unified School District, with help from local businesses and foundations.

Contact: Judy Johnson, Director. (213) 742-7501 or 744-0534.

HUMANITIES FOR ALL: TEACHING THROUGH THEMES

This enrichment program was designed for K–8th grades students, and serves as a model for the development of intercurricular units around themes. The units in the program cover a wide range of topics, including Myths and Fairy Tales; Save Our Earth; Math and Art: A Dynamic Duo; Leaves; Ancient Egypt; and Explorers. It was designed for use in multi-age cooperative groups, but can be adapted to other learning situations, including gifted classes, learning disabled classes, or bi-lingual classes.

Contact Carol Fisher; George Rogers Clark Elementary School; 1045 South Monitor; Chicago, IL 60644; 312-534-6225.

INTEGRATED LIBRARY PROGRAM

Integrated Library Program is one developed for the purpose of helping students improve their research skills, using computers and other library resources. In designing the program, librarians worked with teachers to determine curricular needs of the various departments, and continue working with teacher planning groups to integrate library skills with units being taught in class. The program is housed at Jay High School in San Antonio, TX, and is intended for grades 9–12. It is the goal of the program to integrate research and reference skills, so that students leave school with the ability to access information as it becomes necessary. Funding for computerized research tools was provided by the district.

Contact: Nancy Dobrot, Library Services Coordinator; Northside Independent School District, 5900 Evers Road, San Antonio, TX. 78238. (210) 647-2223.

INTEGRATED STUDIES IN THE MIDDLE GRADES: "DANCING THROUGH WALLS"

Chris Stevenson and Judy Carr, Editors. Teachers College Press. New York. 1993.

INTEGRATED THEMATIC UNITS

Amy Seely. Teacher Created Materials. Westminster, CA. 1995.

INTERDISCIPLINARY CONTOURS: ART, EARTH, SCIENCE, AND LOGO. MCQUADE, F. (SEPTEMBER, 1986). *SCIENCE AND CHILDREN*, *24*(1), 25–27

The author describes a unit of study where children experience a curriculum that integrates earth science, the visual arts, and computer skills to study maps. Additionally, the students create clay environments using topographical features that are plotted on a LOGO program.

INTERDISCIPLINARY CURRICULUM: DESIGN AND IMPLEMENTATION

Heidi Hayes Jacobs. Association for Supervision and Curriculum Development. Alexandria, VA. 1989.

INTERDISCIPLINARY ENGLISH: SCIENCE, TECHNOLOGY, AND SOCIETY. FAGAN, E.R. (1987). *ENGLISH JOURNAL, 76,* 81–83

An interdisciplinary program titled "STS: Science, Technology and Society" is explained in this article. The program is designed to integrate STS with English, using animal issues as the bridge. Students develop an awareness of the connections between humans, animal life, and communication by way of higher level thinking and decision-making activities.

INTERDISCIPLINARY HIGH SCHOOL TEACHING: STRATEGIES FOR INTEGRATED LEARNING

John H. Clarke and Russel M. Agne. Allyn and Bacon, 1997.

INTERDISCIPLINARY TEACHING: WHY AND HOW, 2ND EDITION

Gordon Vars. National Middle School Association. 1993.

INVESTIGATING STREAMS AND RIVERS. AN INTERDISCIPLINARY CURRICULUM GUIDE FOR USE WITH MITCHELL AND STAPP'S "FIELD MANUAL FOR WATER QUALITY MONITORING"

Investigating Streams and Rivers. An Interdisciplinary Curriculum Guide for use with Mitchell and Stapp's "Field Manual for Water Quality Monitoring" is a curriculum designed to develop in secondary students a sense of awareness, concern, and inquiry related to local rivers and streams.

Activities include evaluation of water supplies, exploring rivers, mapping watersheds, identifying potential problems, developing goals, designing a plan of action, and carrying out that plan. The authors, Mare Cromwell and others, are affiliated with GREEN (Global Rivers Environmental Education Network). ERIC Document 361200.

JOURNEYS OF DISCOVERY

Journeys of Discovery is an interdisciplinary curriculum for middle school students based on the travels and discoveries of legendary explorers. Studying the journeys of such famous figures as Marco Polo, Lewis and Clark, and Elanor of Aquitaine and the Crusade of the Kings, students are "invited to become historians, scientists, artists, dramatists, philosophers, and builders in an attempt to transform learning into the active construction of lasting ideas and values." The curriculum was designed by Arthur Ellis of Seattle Pacific University and Richard Scheuerman of St. John's-Endicott School District in Washington State.

Contact: Richard Scheuerman (509) 648-3451 or Arthur Ellis (206) 281-2362.

LANGUAGE DEVELOPMENT THROUGH HOLISTIC LEARNING (MATHEMATICS, ART, SCIENCE, TECHNOLOGY, AND EDUCATION RESOURCES) BERNEY, T.D. & BARRERA, M. (1988–89)

This paper describes the evaluation of "Project MASTER" (math, art, science, technology, and educational resources), a program designed to help Spanish speaking students develop their English skills. Science serves as the foundation for connecting communication skills in English and mathematics, and in computer and higher level thinking skills. This paper can be accessed through:

ERIC Document 319253.

LEARNING AND LOVING IT: THEME STUDIES IN THE CLASSROOM

Ruth Gamberg and others. Heinemann. Portsmouth, NH. 1988.

NATIONAL MIDDLE SCHOOL ASSOCIATION / NATIONAL ASSOCIATION OF SECONDARY SCHOOL PRINCIPALS

National Middle School Association 2600 Corporate Executive Drive, #370, Columbus, Ohio, 43231. 614-895-4730. National Association of Secondary School Principals 1904 Association Drive, Reston, VA, 22091. 703-866-0200. These are excellent resources for exploring the variety of interdisciplinary themes and programs that are currently being taught in middle schools and secondary schools across the country. The following publication is the work of the National Middle School Association and Prentice Hall.

ABSTRACTS OF AWARD-WINNING PROJECTS FOR THE MIDDLE GRADES. 1995 AND 1996 TEAM TEACHING AWARDS

Prentice Hall and the National Middle School Association have published this booklet of 20 summaries of award-winning interdisciplinary projects dealing with a variety of themes, including cultures, natural disasters, and the environment. Each project is described briefly and lists a contact person should an interested educator desire more information. Contact: Prentice Hall School Division, Upper Saddle River, NJ and Needham, MA.

Seven examples of award-winning projects follow.

CONSTRUCTING THE AMERICAN DREAM

This month-long interdisciplinary unit is designed to help students explore the world of economics, career decisions, and personal choices in terms of budgeting money and home ownership. The unit involves three seminars in the subject areas of English, math, and art. The first of these seminars, titled "Careers, Choice or Chance?" allows students to practice making career choices through activities such as interviewing for a job and applying for a car loan. "Banking, Balancing, and Budgeting", the second seminar, focuses on check writing and balancing books, and the third seminar has students exploring housing design, construction, costs, and careers in architecture.

Contact: Milwee Middle School, Longwood, Florida; 407-831-4122.

CRIME SCENE INVESTIGATION

This is an interdisciplinary project designed for eighth graders and integrates English, science, government, social studies, art, speech, and drama. Students investigate a possible "crime" that has occurred at the school, and in carrying out their investigation, they develop such science skills as organizing, classifying, and drawing conclusions, as well as English skills such as writing technical reports and studying handwriting samples. An important part of the project is the study of the Constitution, the Bill of Rights, and the different branches of government to better understand how the legal system works. The project culminates with a trial, where students participate as defense and prosecuting teams, court reporters, clerks, and bailiffs. Contact: Woodrow Wilson Middle School, Glendale, California; 818-244-8145.

JOURNEYS HOME

This interdisciplinary unit was developed to explore World War II as it was experienced by Americans and foreigners living here at the time the war took place. Through Language Arts, Math, and Science classes, students not only learn the factual information about World War II, but also develop a sense of empathy for those who experienced the war in some way. By interviewing people in the community about their experiences during the war, students gain a deeper understanding of life during a world war.

Contact: Barrington Middle School, Barrington, Rhode Island; 401-247-3160.

OCEANS OF OPPORTUNITY

Teachers involved in this interdisciplinary unit combine their efforts around the BOC International solo sailing competition. Students participate in Language Arts, Social Studies, Science, Math, and Art lessons to learn about oceans, sailing, maps and research skills, weather patterns, safety and survival considerations, and the art forms of different ports-of-call. Both traditional and alternative forms of assessment are used to evaluate student learning.

Contact: Cowpens Middle School, Cowpen, South Carolina; 864-463-3310.

TO-BACCO OR NOT TO-BACCO: A HOT ISSUE

This four-week interdisciplinary unit, designed for seventh grade students, is intended to explore the economic, ethical, and personal rights issues related to the use of tobacco. The history of tobacco and its impact on the economy is studied in Social Studies, while in Language Arts, students interview both users and non-users of tobacco products. In addition, advertising related to tobacco products is examined. In Math, students determine the monthly and yearly costs associated with tobacco use, and in Science they study the effect of tobacco on the body's organs, among other activities.

Contact: Johnson Traditional Middle School, Louisville, Kentucky; 502-485-8277.

UNDERSTANDING THE ELDERLY AND THE AGING PROCESS

The goal of this unit is to help students understand the social and physical aspects of aging through reading, writing, wellness, nutrition, and community outreach activities. Besides reading novels, poems, and essays about the dimensions of aging, students do research on diseases affecting the elderly such as Alzheimer's, heart disease, arthritis, and arteriosclerosis. Students also "adopt" a local senior citizen, exchanging both school and home visits. The unit is designed for sixth grade, and is taught by a four member team of teachers.

Contact: Dublin Middle School, Dublin, Virginia; 540-674-4663.

VOICES AND VISIONS: PIKES'S PEAK WOMEN OF THE TWENTIETH CENTURY

The goal of this year-long project is to gather oral histories from elderly local women so that students might learn first hand about the multicultural heritage of western communities. The project integrates social studies and English in the study of state history, oral biographies, the contributions and difficulties of pioneers, and play writing based on primary resources. The project culminates in the presentation of a play, written by students, which pieces together the history and experiences shared in the oral biographies.

Contact: Eagleview Middle School, Colorado Springs, Colorado; 719-548-0316.

PLANNING INTEGRATED CURRICULUM: THE CALL TO ADVENTURE

Susan M. Drake. Association for Supervision and Curriculum Development. 1993.

PLANNING WHEELS TURN CURRICULUM AROUND. PALMER, J. (1991). *EDUCATIONAL LEADERSHIP, 49* (2). P. 57–60

This article describes a system used in the Maryland Public Schools, Howard County, to create interdisciplinary curricula. Two examples of planning wheels are included: "Smoke-Free 2000" and "Consumerism".

RESTRUCTURING FOR AN INTERDISCIPLINARY CURRICULUM

John M. Jenkins and Daniel Tanner, Editors. National Association of Secondary School Principals. Reston, VA. 1992.

SQUALLS ON THE NISQUALLY: A SIMULATION GAME. OCEAN RELATED CURRICULUM ACTIVITIES

Squalls on the Nisqually: A Simulation Game. Ocean Related Curriculum Activities, written by Andrea Marrett, is one of several interdisciplinary programs developed by Project ORCA (Ocean Related Curriculum Activities) to increase awareness of the relationship between humans and the oceans. Each curriculum packet contains activities and lessons designed to explore a specific topic related to oceans, marine life, the environment, and the role humans play in using and caring for these resources. The curriculum packets are appropriate for various different grade levels, and target teachers in Washington State. This particular curriculum is based on a simulation game in which the students make decisions about land use in a coastal zone environment. Other titles in the program series include: Tools of Oceanography (Florence Sands), High Tide, Low Tide (Gloria Snively), and Energy from the Sea (Claire Jones). The Pacific Science Center in Seattle, the University of Washington, the Washington Sea Grant Program, and NOAA are affiliated with and sponsors of the program.

ERIC Document 289683.

TEACHING U.S. HISTORY IN THE ELEMENTARY SCHOOL: AN INTERDISCIPLINARY APPROACH

Teaching U.S. History in the Elementary School: An Interdisciplinary Approach is a curricular program edited by Laurie Singleton, in conjunction with the Social Science Education Consortium in Boulder, Colorado, which attempts to integrate the history of science, technology, art, religion, and society with United States history. The 30 lessons help the learner make connections between periods in American history and the related social, political, economic, and cultural events of the time.

ERIC Document 365589.

THE COMPLETE GUIDE TO THEMATIC UNITS: CREATING THE INTEGRATED CURRICULUM

Anita Meyer Meinbach, Liz Rothlein, and Anthony Fredericks. Christopher-Gordon. Norwood, MA. 1995.

THE CORE TEACHER: GORDON VARS, EDITOR

This newsletter is a service of the National Association for Core Curriculum, and is devoted to information related to interdisciplinary studies, core curriculum, unified studies, and other integrative and interdisciplinary programs.

Contact: National Association for Core Curriculum, 1100 East Summit Street, #5, Kent, Ohio. 44240-4094.

THE INTERDISCIPLINARY TEACHER'S HANDBOOK: INTEGRATED TEACHING ACROSS THE CURRICULUM

Stephen Tchudi and Stephen Lafer. Heinemann. Portsmouth, NH. 1996.

THEMATIC UNITS: AN INTEGRATED APPROACH TO TEACHING SCIENCE AND SOCIAL STUDIES

Anthony Fredericks, Anita Meyer Meinbach, and Liz Rothlein. Harper Collins. New York. 1993.

THEME IMMERSION: INQUIRY-BASED CURRICULUM IN ELEMENTARY AND MIDDLE SCHOOLS

Maryann Manning, Gary Manning, and Roberta Long. Heinemann. Portsmouth, NH. 1994.

THE MINDFUL SCHOOL: HOW TO INTEGRATE THE CURRICULA

Robin Fogarty. Skylight Publishing. Palatine, IL. 1991

THE NATIONAL CENTER FOR CROSS-DISCIPLINARY TEACHING AND LEARNING

Sponsored by the College Board, the Center publishes a newsletter with articles on research, reports on policy development, and profiles of best practices in cross-disciplinary studies. Contact: The College Board, 45 Columbus Avenue, New York, New York 10023-6992.

THE PAGEANT OF THE ARTS: AN INTEGRATED ARTS PROGRAM. BLAYDES, JOHN (JUNE, 1991), *COMMUNICATOR*, *21*, P.16–17

In this article, Blaydes discusses the Pageants interdisciplinary program, which gives students in-depth arts experiences in an attempt to uncover creative abilities and foster self-esteem.

TRASH CONFLICTS: A SCIENCE AND SOCIAL STUDIES CURRICULUM ON THE ETHICS OF DISPOSAL, AN INTERDISCIPLINARY CURRICULUM

Trash Conflicts: A Science and Social Studies Curriculum on the Ethics of Disposal, An Interdisciplinary Curriculum is a curriculum that integrates science, mathematics, and language in an attempt to develop an awareness of the social and scientific issues surrounding waste disposal. Students investigate controversies concerning waste disposal, hazardous waste problems, social justice and waste disposal, and methods of disposal. Activities allow students to experiment with waste disposal methods in the classroom and to develop plans for making a difference in the waste disposal problem. Amy Ballin and others authored the curriculum, under the affiliation of Educators for Social Responsibility, Cambridge, MA.

ERIC Document 372982.

WRITING ACROSS THE CURRICULUM

Writing Across the Curriculum is a program intended to extend the improvement of students' writing skills in all areas of the curriculum; that is, the process of writing is developed in all subject areas. Feedback on student writing assignments is given by graduate students from the University of Minnesota, which was a partner in designing the program. Funded by Apple Computers (technology donations) and US West, the project encourages students to write more, both in terms of quantity and quality, through the use of technology and feedback. The program has been conducted at Totino-Grace High School, Fridley, MN.

Contact: Richard Paul, Mary Ellen Briel, Dennis Cooney, or Peggy Anderson (612) 571-9116.

6

A Glossary of Useful Terms

BLOCK SCHEDULING

Block scheduling and related terms are generic phrases used to describe the practice of scheduling classes, usually at the junior or senior high school level, over longer periods of time. The reasoning behind this type of scheduling is the belief that the traditional 45-50 minute class periods do not allow time for students to deal with topics in-depth or to work on projects together with other students or individually, particularly in classes such as the science labs.

The practice usually takes one of two forms. In some block classes students are taught the same subject by the teacher for lengthened periods of time, typically around 90 minutes. For example, an algebra class may meet 90 minutes a day for a semester, thus putting in the equivalent of one full year's course time in a single semester. With this model students take half the typical number of courses each semester. Variations of this model exist which extend the course of study over the entire year, with students taking the normal number of courses per semester. Courses may meet for the extended periods two days one week and three days the next week over the entire year, or there may be Monday/Wednesday extended period classes, Tuesday/Thursday extended period classes, with all classes meeting for shortened or regular length on Fridays.

A second form of block scheduling may follow any of the above organization, but differs in that two or more subjects may be combined to form an integrated *or interdisciplinary curriculum.*

BRAINSTORMING

Brainstorming is a technique in which participants suggest as many thoughts, ideas, solutions, etc. to a problem or issue as they possibly can. Brainstorming is to be conducted in a spirit of openness so that no judgments or critiques are allowed. Quantity of input is valued over quality. The idea is to place on the table as many thoughts as possible, so that as later phases of *problem-solving* occur there is some assurance that a wide range of options was at least initially considered.

BROAD-FIELDS CURRICULUM

Broad-fields curriculum refers to a pattern of curriculum organization that seeks to unify separate subjects, downplaying their separate identities and concentrating instead on integrative themes, such as "Saving the Rainforests," or "The Westward Movement." Broad-fields approaches are usually identified with project learning and collaborative activities such as pageants, fairs, displays, etc. A common criticism of the broad-fields approach is that the systematic treatment of *basic skills* is often missing or deficient and that students seldom delve deeply enough into a given discipline to master its content, skills, and ideas.

CHILD-CENTERED CURRICULUM

The key to child-centered curriculum is the growth and development of the individual. The premise is that true learning is spontaneous, emotionally-invested, and cannot be prepackaged, and that people learn best when they can decide what to learn for themselves. Meaningful learning results from individual exploration, investigation, and choosing what to learn. Believers in child-centered curriculum feel that time spent in school learning someone else's knowledge results in several serious deficiencies: lack of self-understanding; lack of interest; lack of meaning.

CITIZENSHIP EDUCATION

Citizenship is considered one of the primary goals of American public education. Although citizenship education is most often associated with the social studies curriculum, there is an implicit charge for the school as a whole and for each curricular area to support the goal of citizenship. A problem identified by a number of critics is that no common definition of citizenship education is to be found. Thus citizenship education is a goal in totalitarian societies as well as in democratic societies, so it could scarcely signify the same thing even though the word is used commonly. Civic education, a closely related term, was one of the *Seven Cardinal Principles of Secondary Education*, formulated in 1918. Today, however, civic education has come to be more closely identified with the discipline-related study of informed participation in a democratic society.

CONCEPT MAP (CONCEPT MAPPING)

A person's graphic, diagrammatic, or schematic representation of his or her understanding of a concept is referred to as a concept map. Construction of a concept map allows a learner to represent his/her level of knowledge of a concept in question while illustrating the concept's larger context in a web of related schematic knowledge. Thus a map of the concept "element" might illustrate not only its properties but its place in the context of atoms, molecules, other elements, and compounds.

CONSTRUCTIONISM

The term contructionism (not to be confused with *constructivism*) is one used by Professor Seymour Papert of MIT as a key ingredient of student-centered learning. Constructionism is based on the assumption that students will do best by finding for themselves the specific knowledge they need. The teacher's role is to help students by ensuring that they are supported morally, psychologically, materially, and intellectually. As the term itself suggests, constructionism emphasizes the learner as a constructor in the most literal sense, for example, using Legos, kitchen materials such as recipes to make cakes, etc. Papert's idea is that the construction that takes place in the head is often greatly facilitated by construction of a more tangible kind, whether a sand castle, a poem, a model, and so on.

CONSTRUCTIVISM

Constructivism refers to a theory that learners construct their own knowledge and therefore their version of reality from their own unique experiences. It is this "construction" or schema that a learner then uses to accommodate and assimilate any new experience. The process of knowledge construction is thought to be an active one. Because of the complexities inherent in any real experience and because each learner's prior construction is unique, what someone learns in a given situation is often unpredictable.

COOPERATIVE LEARNING

Cooperative learning is an approach to the teaching/learning process which has been proposed as a viable alternative to the current individualistic and competitive practices of schools. There are several forms of cooperative learning, but they all involve students working in groups or teams to achieve certain educational goals. Its proponents propose it as a generic strategy that could be used in any setting, while others have designed subject-matter specific strategies. Cooperative learning is not a peculiarly American educational phenomenon. It is touted from Israel to New Zealand, from Sweden to Japan.

The research claims that detail the elements of cooperative learning are more elaborate and documented than those of any other movement in education today. Study after study finds its way into the scholarly journals. Literally hundreds of articles, from research to practice, appear annually on this topic. All the major professional subject matter associations have published special editions showing how cooperative learning can be used in mathematics, social studies, language arts, science, etc.

Cooperative learning takes on many different forms in classrooms, but they all involve students working in groups or teams to achieve certain educational goals. Beyond the most basic premise of working together, students must also depend on each other, a concept called *positive interdependence*. From here cooperative learning takes on specific traits advocated differentially by different developers. In some cases, cooperative learning is conceived of as a generic strategy that one could use in practically any setting or in any course of study. In other cases, cooperative learning is conceived of as a subject-matter specific strategy.

Various models of cooperative learning exist. David and Roger Johnson of the University of Minnesota are the authors of the *Learning Together* model. The model is based in a generic group process theory applicable to all disciplines and grade levels. Students are placed in formal or informal base groups which are charged with solving problems, discussing issues, carrying out projects, etc. Robert Slavin of Johns Hopkins University has developed a cooperative learning model called *Student Team Learning*. His model is less generic than that of the Johnsons. In fact, it has at least four permutations, each of which is specifically designed to address different concerns. Other notable models include that of Shlomo and Yael Sharan of Israel, which is a general plan for organizing a classroom using a variety of cooperative tactics for different disciplines; that of Spencer Kagan, whose Structural Approach includes such intriguing procedures as Roundrobin, Corners, Numbered Head Together, Roundtable, and Match Mine; and Elliot Aronson's Jigsaw, composed of interdependent learning teams for academic content applicable to various age groups.

Used properly, cooperative learning is designed to supplement and complement direct instruction and the other teaching/learning activities typical of classroom life. Its main function is to replace much of the individual, often competitive seatwork that so dominates American classrooms. It should be noted, as well, that advocates of cooperative learning are not necessarily opposed to individualistic and competitive learning. Their opposition is to its near complete dominance. Most cooperative learning advocates will say that there is a time and place for each type of learning, but that there must be considerably more cooperative learning in classrooms than is presently the case.

CORE CURRICULUM

The core curriculum, as originally conceived in the 1930s, was proposed as an interdisciplinary approach relating one subject to another in the study of significant issues. The most common tactic was to "correlate" English/language arts with history/social studies. The content of the core was taught in an extended block of time centered around socially relevant issues, with a special emphasis on group work and projects. The idea of unit teaching and learning is commonly identified with core curriculum. The central themes undergirding the core curriculum approach were invariably that of life adjustment and citizenship in a democracy. In more recent times, the core has come to be identified with the *middle school* curriculum and the large blocks of time devoted to integrated studies.

In addition to retaining much of its former flavor, core curriculum has also been influenced by the reports of various commissions which advocate a required minimum number of subjects that all students in the system are required to learn. Ernest Boyer, for example, has proposed a "core of common learning" consisting of 14.5 units, and the National Commission on Excellence proposed a recommended core of 13.5 units which comprise the "five new basics" thus the term is probably as confusing as it is helpful in light of its considerable evolution and its considerably different meanings which range from a *progressive* to a *back-to-basics* orientation.

CRITICAL THINKING

Critical thinking is a generic term used to describe a host of mental processes that are thought to be "different" from simply remembering or explaining. Various terms are used for critical thinking, including higher order thinking skills, problem solving skills, strategic reasoning skills, productive thinking skills, etc. They all are used more or less interchangeably, and all imply that these mental "skills" are located at a higher place on some taxonomic register and ought not, therefore, be confused with lower level thinking skills. Virtually every set of state or educational goals contain some reference to the desire of developing these skills in students. Specific terms used for these skills may include broad areas, such as application, analysis, synthesis, evaluation, decision-making, problem solving, conceptualizing, and information processing. More specific skills may also be specified, such as identifying alternatives, extrapolation, determining factual accuracy, and detecting bias.

There are, however, several problems which seem to be endemic to the entire area labeled "thinking skills." For starters, there is little agreement about what thinking skills are. Virtually every program or curriculum has a list of skills to be developed, but the concepts are quite abstract in many cases with a range of definitions applied to any given thinking skill. For example, "classification" is often identified as an important thinking skill because it is so associated with scientific thought and expression. But what is meant by the term "classification?" Putting things in groups? Organizing whole taxonomies? Recognizing that different attributes lead one to assign something to a particular category? This is very vexing because "classification" is a rather concrete skill compared to, say, "evaluation" or "analysis."

Another problem is that of measuring thinking skills. Measuring academic achievement, the mastery of single digit multiplication for example, is relatively simple, but it is next to impossible get *valid* and *reliable* measures of such abstract constructs, and when the tests that are available have no agreed-on definition of the skills.

Whether thinking skills can be taught successfully to students independent of content remains a matter of some debate. Most experts have concluded that they cannot. So the issue of transfer becomes paramount. Can someone who has been taught how to predict use "prediction" as a generic skill applicable to literature, geography, personal problems, etc.? Probably not. And how does one teach others to predict, assuming that we agree on its importance as a thinking skill? Predictions, after all, can be based on evidence as well as on intuition.

Another issue is that of a huge assumption which may in fact not be warranted, the assumption that teachers themselves possess these various thinking skills. If they do not, how could they possibly teach them? In his book, *A Place Called School*, researcher John Goodlad speculates that one reason he never saw teachers teaching concepts could be because they themselves do not think conceptually. The extent to which teachers have these skills and are prepared to model or teach them is largely unknown.

Lastly, we know very little about how people think. We know much more about the products of someone's thoughts than we know about how he/she arrives at those products. There is some considerable debate about whether thinking is a conscious or an unconscious process. So if we are not sure how people think, how can we proceed with the business of teaching them how to think in such a way that is compatible with given individuals' styles or approaches to situations that demand thinking?

All of this notwithstanding, there seems to be no shortage of people willing to jump into the breech. Programs abound, and the thinking skills movement is going full-force across the country. A useful paradigm for considering these matters is offered by Ronald Brandt. He describes teaching **for** thinking as the engagement of content and learning activities and development of language and conceptual abilities through teacher questioning, student-to-student interaction, group discussions, etc. Brandt identifies teaching **about** thinking as encouraging students to be aware of their thinking, reflecting on it, and learning to control it. Students are asked to monitor their own thinking and to make deliberate use of various thinking frames. Brandt suggests that teaching **of** thinking represents the attempt to teach particular mental skills such as summarizing, paraphrasing, and decision-making. This last concern is no doubt the weakest area, and the one we know least about.

There are a number of commercial thinking skills programs purchased and used by schools, and some districts develop their own. In both cases there is little, if any, evidence that such programs actually improve student thinking. At this time we would say that the decision to purchase one of these programs and to invest teachers' time in inservice training cannot be made rationally based on the research evidence. However, there is so much in the way of interesting, intriguing activities in the various thinking skills programs and may enhance existing teaching strategies.

CROSS-AGE TUTORING

Cross-age tutoring refers to the practice of assigning older students to work with younger students, often tutoring them in academic subjects or skills such as reading or math. This may take one of two forms. In some places, all older students regardless of achievement level or accomplishment are assigned to work with younger students. This arrangement is thought to aid both parties, providing assistance and individualized instruction to younger students, while helping older students to solidify their own knowledge and to understand and care for those younger. Another common practice is to assign older students who are at risk of dropping out of school to work with younger students with the belief that such involvement will improve the older students skills and self-esteem, reducing the likelihood of that student dropping out of school.

CURRICULUM

The term "curriculum" derives from Latin roots, and its literal meaning is that of a running course or race track. Thus its application to education and to life in schools is metaphorical, but it signifies the course of study that students follow toward the completion of a program, diploma, or degree. Because of its rather cryptic and symbolic meaning, the term curriculum has been subject to many definitions and interpretations. Most typically, the term refers to the formal designation of that which is taught at school. Many have distinguished between the formal curriculum and the *hidden curriculum*. The formal curriculum is the obvious, published course of study offered by a school. The hidden curriculum represents those socializing, experiential elements that happen along the way.

Some interesting arguments exist over exactly what the curriculum is. Traditionalists think of the curriculum as being found in textbooks, lectures, and other expert sources. This is to say that the curriculum is pre-existent to the learner's encounter with it. The task of the learner is to master the elements of knowledge, skills, and values contained in the curriculum. Such a curriculum is usually represented by a published scope, that is, *what* is to be taught, and sequence, that is, the *order* in which things are to be taught. Recently much criticism has been brought to bear on such a view. *Constructivists,* for example, argue that each person must construct his/her own curriculum based on individual perceptions, the unique knowledge of a given individual, and the making of meaning which flows from the encounter with ideas and the perceptions of others. In other words, such a curriculum cannot be pre-existent; rather it is emergent and always subjective. This argument has actually been around in one form or another for some time, and John Dewey once attempted to resolve it by stating that the child and the curriculum were one and the same thing.

DIRECT INSTRUCTION

Direct instruction is a teaching method that places the center of gravity with the teacher, with the teacher typically instructing a whole class. The two most common forms of direct instruction are lecturing and explaining. Other forms include recitation or question asking and class discussion led by the teacher. Because the approach is teacher-centered, much research has been conducted in order to derive principles of effective teaching, especially the teaching of basic skills and knowledge with which direct instruction is so closely identified. The term direct instruction was coined by Barak Rosenshine who wrote:

> "Direct instruction refers to academically focused, teacher-directed classrooms using sequenced and structured materials. It refers to teaching activities where goals are clear to students, time allocated for instruction is sufficient and continuous, coverage of content is extensive, the performance of students is monitored . . . and feedback to students is immediate and academically oriented. In direct instruction the teacher controls instructional goals, chooses materials appropriate for the student's ability, and paces the instructional episode." (1979, p. 38)

One of the best known, perhaps the best known and used, examples of direct instruction is Madeline Hunter's *ITIP* or *Mastery Teaching Program*. Hunter's approach emphasizes teaching to an objective, set induction, review, guided practice, checking for understanding, and monitoring and adjusting.

Rosenshine, B. (1979). *Content, time, and direct instruction. In P. Peterson and H. Walberg (Eds.), Research on teaching: Concepts, findings, and implications (pp. 28-56).* Berkeley: McCutchan. quoted in Woolfolk, A. (1995). *Educational psychology, 6th edition,* Needham Heights, MA: Simon and Schuster.

DISCOVERY LEARNING

Discovery learning is a teaching/learning approach based on inductive thinking, popularized in the 1960s by the cognitive psychologist Jerome Bruner and others. In discovery learning, students work on their own to discover basic principles. In a science class, students might be encouraged to investigate animal behavior in order to reach inferences about diet, feeding patterns, etc. Discovery learning invariably involves asking questions, exploration, data gathering, concluding, and generalizing. Advocates of discovery learning generally point to the process of acquiring knowledge as coequal with the product or answer itself. It is their contention that students must experience the process of how knowledge is created in order to better understand information, ideas, and skills. Discovery learning fits quite naturally into the progressive stream of educational thought in that it shifts the center of gravity from teacher to student, making the student an active learner. Discovery learning is sometimes divided into pure discovery, which means giving students minimal structure or cues and guided discovery, which gives the teacher a more prominent role in asking questions, providing cues, materials, etc.

FORMATIVE ASSESSMENT

Assessment strategies that are used during the planning and implementation stages of a new program. Most often associated with *evaluation research*, the purpose of formative assessment is to plan for and provide feedback during a process. For example, if a school is implementing a new ninety-minute block schedule for the first time, formative assessment would take place early in the implementation to provide feedback to the participants on how it is working and what may need modification in order to enhance its chance of success. Formative assessment is sometimes referred to as *process assessment* because much of the evaluation activities are concerned with the process of implementation. Data collected may be quantitative in nature, but many times is more informal in the form of participant comments, observations, and analyses. Such feedback is useful for making changes in the program to enhance the chances of success. Formative assessment should be followed by *summative assessment*, research designed to assess the effectiveness of a program after it has been completed. When the concept of formative assessment is applied to a classroom setting it may be thought of as the feedback a teacher receives from a student during a lesson that instructs the teacher as to whether or not a modification of the lesson is needed to enhance instructional effectiveness.

INTERDISCIPLINARY STUDIES

Interdisciplinary studies and related terms are used somewhat interchangeably to indicate the bringing together of separate disciplines around common themes, issues, or problems. Based in progressive educational thought, interdisciplinary studies involve teacher teaming, students working together, real-world applications, and active, experiential learning.

The main arguments for interdisciplinary curriculums, or integrated studies as they are sometimes called, are twofold: 1) the knowledge explosion is very real and there is simply too much information to be covered in the curriculum, and 2) most school subjects are taught to students in isolation from other, potentially related, subjects. By combining subjects around themes or projects, a certain economy is achieved because much of the repetitious material that occurs from subject to subject is eliminated. And when subjects are connected, students begin to see meaningful relationships because the subject matter serves as a vehicle for learning rather than as an end in itself. These are among the primary claims of the advocates of interdisciplinary curriculum. Among the improvements which supposedly follow suit when a change to interdisciplinary curriculum is made are heightened teacher collaboration, greater student involvement, higher level thinking, better content mastery, real-world applications, and fewer fragmented learning experiences. Most teachers and administrators dream of these outcomes, so the claims tend to be rather attractive.

Integrating curriculum is not a new idea. The learning done in most "natural" situations including apprenticeships, for example, tends to be interdisciplinary. Language arts and social studies, "subjects" taken for granted in today's elementary curriculum, are themselves interdisciplinary versions of several former separate subjects. And at the secondary level, many districts have for several years integrated their mathematics programs, shucking off the old algebra/geometry/advanced algebra sequence. But the current trend goes somewhat further than the prior attempts to coalesce, say, history and the social sciences into something called social studies. The movement today is dedicated to crossing new frontiers between and among school subjects.

A criticism of interdisciplinary curricula is one that is obvious to any *essentialist*. Because the units are teacher/student developed, they tend to have a seemingly random flavor. The essentialist's need for an orderly scope and sequence is not met to say the least. To interdisciplinary advocates, who tend to be progressives, this is the beauty of such a curriculum. It is fair to say, however, that interdisciplinary curricula often tend to favor social studies, language arts, and the arts while slighting mathematics, and this a serious problem. It is not insoluble, but it is difficult to overcome.

There is also a phenomenon known as "the tyranny of integration." Sometimes teachers become so committed to integrated studies that they find themselves trying to integrate everything they teach. This can quickly lead to a different kind of artificiality. The fact of the matter is that not everything probably can or should be integrated. Matters of discretion become paramount when such factors are weighed. The simple idea that is too easily lost sight of is that integration is a **means** to an end and not an end in itself.

Proponents of the interdisciplinary curriculum cite many advantages. Most common are the beliefs that interdisciplinary curriculum improves higher level thinking skills, that learning is less fragmented, that students are provided with a more coherent set of learning experiences and therefore with a more unified sense of process and content, that interdisciplinary curriculum provides real world applications, hence heightening the opportunity for transfer of learning, that improved mastery of content results from interdisciplinary learning, that interdisciplinary learning experiences positively shape a learner's overall approach to knowledge, and that motivation to learn is improved in interdisciplinary settings.

Opponents of the interdisciplinary approach point out that their is very little or no evidence at all to substantiate the above claims, which there isn't. They also question that content mastery takes place because much of what passes off as interdisciplinary is really **non**-disciplinary in nature.

INTEREST

The term "interest" is often used by developmentalists to mean an approach to the curriculum whereby the learner makes decisions about what to study based on what he/she is interested in. Purists are careful to point out that interest should not be confused with curiosity or other superficial inclinations. In an interest-based approach to learning, it is incumbent upon the teacher to study students and to know them well in order to support their learning interests. But ultimately, the student's innate desire to learn is the key to growth and development. The Doctrine of Interest was originally proclaimed by the Roman orator and rhetorician Quintilian in the first century A.D. He boldly suggested that children ought to study the things they are interested in because forced learning yielded little result. The idea was refined in the 18th century by Jean Rousseau who wrote that students ought to study what they want to study, but they should want to study what the teacher wants them to study. Of course, Rousseau was saying that teaching and learning ought to be a relational endeavor. John Dewey invoked the idea of interest, contrasting it with effort, or disciplined acts of the will in study, in his book *Interest and Effort in Education.*

JIGSAW

Jigsaw is a *cooperative learning* technique developed by Elliot Aronson which employs interdependent learning teams for academic content applicable to various age groups. Typically, students engaged in a jigsaw activity bring specific "pieces" of information or skills to their cooperative group, and each student shares with or peer teaches the others until the whole learning entity is complete.

JOPLIN PLAN

The Joplin plan is a system of instructional grouping in graded schools that regroups students, generally for part of the school day, on the basis of a single ability, irrespective of the grade level or age of the student. For example, all students in an elementary school who are reading at the 3rd grade level or below would go to a particular teacher's room for reading instruction only.

LEARNING

We can say that learning has taken place when someone knows something, can do something, or feels differently as a result of experience, either direct or vicarious. It is easy to lose sight of the simple fact that school is not about teaching, which is merely a means to an end. School is about learning, especially about learning knowledge, skills, and values in relational settings. Of course, what is learned at school includes the intentioned and the unintentional, the planned and the incidental. But always, learning involves change: change in ability, in knowledge, in perspective, and in one's sense of self and others.

LEARNING CENTERS

Learning centers are a means of organizing a classroom in such a way that students can concentrate on an area of interest at a specific site dedicated to that pursuit. For example, in a primary classroom one might find centers roughly corresponding to school subjects (sometimes called stations) scattered about the room. An arts center might include materials and space for drawing, painting, sculpting, etc. A reading center might have a bookshelf full of good books and magazines, a carpet, and a couple of comfortable chairs where children can go to read. A science center may consist of a table with gadgets, science books, a place to experiment, etc. Learning centers are most commonly associated with child-centered approaches to the curriculum. The student learns as much as is reasonably possible on the basis of personal choice, and the teacher's role is that of facilitator and mediator of learning as well as organizer of the learning environment.

LEARNING STYLES

Learning styles represent the consistent pattern of behaviors that can be associated with each individual as he/she approaches and interprets a learning experience. The basic research of this area is found in brain research and personality types. A number of models of learning styles have been proposed by individuals such as Rita and Kenneth Dunn, Marie Carbo, and Herman Witkin. *Field dependent/field independent*, abstract/concrete, and visual/auditory/kinesthetic/tactile are just of a few of the styles which have purported to have been identified. Each of these styles have implications for how students should be taught, and each have strong advocates and inservice/training programs and materials available to schools.

The thesis of learning styles is that individuals vary considerably in how they learn. This is to say that any given person has what are called modality strengths that are, one supposes, determined by a combination of hereditary and environmental influences. These modality strengths, which translate into preferences to learn and communicate visually, orally, spatially, tactily, etc., are one's learning style. Beyond that there are some further considerations, for example, whether one learns better in a quiet or busy setting, a formal or relaxed environment, or together or alone.

It has been suggested that learning styles are not merely a phenomenon of individual differences but that differences are also found among and between cultures. For example, some have claimed that Native American students rely more on visually perceived stimuli and tend to learn better in their natural settings experientially, while African American students tend to be field dependent learners which means that they tend to take their cues from the social environment and that much of their motivation comes from factors external to the material to be learned itself. Added to the cultural dimension is that of social class as a factor in determining how one learns.

It is common to categorize learning styles into some type of taxonomy of human characteristics of learning behavior. The various taxonomies include cognitive, affective, and physiological considerations. Thus with respect to cognition, a person might exhibit concrete or abstract learning characteristics. With respect to affect, a person might find quite different sources for his/her motivation to learn. And with respect to physiological considerations, a person might have preferences for different light, temperature, and room arrangement. For each of these areas there are a number of instruments that claim to assess a person's style.

The essence of learning styles is that each of us receives and processes information differently, and because this is so teachers should make every attempt to know how students learn best. The logic of this thought dictates to us that all styles are equal and that intelligence and ability are equally but differentially distributed among human beings. Typical school assignments tend to discriminate in favor or against certain learners. But the issue may not be one of ability if one person learns much and another little from, say, a particular lecture. It may be, rather, that the lecture format was more suited to one person's learning style than to another's. What this says is that otherwise capable people are left behind in many cases simply because the approach to learning was inappropriate, not because they were incapable of learning the idea.

The relationship between various learning styles and ability to learn subject matter is not well established. It tends to remain, in our opinion, within the realm of speculation. Witkin, a pioneer researcher in this field, maintained that any given style is not superior to another, a proposition that immediately intersects with our ideas of the definition of intelligence. But the problem with this is that the very definition of intelligence is being thoughtfully re-examined by such researchers as Howard Gardner and the chances are that what we presently mean by intelligence as measured by IQ tests and what we will mean by intelligence in the future are two different things. At present analytical abilities are considered basic to one's intelligence as measured by IQ tests. Global, intuitive learners tend to score much lower on tests of analytical abilities. Are they therefore less intelligent than analytical thinkers who obviously score higher? Well, it depends on one's definition of intelligence.

Many outside the movement are critical of the research used to support learning styles. The criticisms include the following points:

1. The validity and reliability of the instruments are questionable, and many learning styles theorists have not distinguished the learning styles constructs from intelligence.
2. The experimental designs employed in classroom-based learning styles research are weak to non-existent with inadequate controls.

3. Bias on the part of the researchers, possibly due to "mercenary" interests in learning styles results.
4. The Hawthorne Effect generated by the enthusiasm of doing something new may explain some of the results.

LEARNING TOGETHER

Learning Together is a cooperative learning model developed by David and Roger Johnson of the University of Minnesota. The model is based in a generic group process theory applicable to all disciplines and grade levels. Students are placed in formal or informal base groups which are charged with solving problems, discussing issues, carrying out projects, etc. The Johnson and Johnson model is built on five elements which trace back to the theories of Morton Deutsch. The first element is *positive interdependence* in which students must believe that they are linked with other students to the point that they cannot succeed unless the other students also succeed. The second element is that of *face-to-face* interaction in which students must converse with each other, helping one another with the learning tasks, problems, and novel ideas. The third element is *individual accountability* in which each student must be held accountable for his/her performance with the results given to both the individual and the group. The fourth element is *social skills* in which students are taught and must use appropriate group interaction skills as part of the learning process. The fifth element is *group processing* of goal achievement in which student groups must regularly monitor what they are accomplishing and how the group and individuals might function more effectively. Teachers must be trained in these elements, and they must be able to teach them to their students in turn.

LITERACY

Literacy is generally meant to describe a level of reading, writing, and communication abilities that permit an individual to learn through print modalities as well as through electronic means. Primarily, a person can be considered literate in a functional sense if he/she can complete an application form, read a newspaper, do the level of calculations needed to keep a checkbook, etc. For children and secondary students, the same idea obtains, but it is merely scaled down against norms for the given age level. Functional literacy can be thought of as "entry level" literacy. At a higher level, one is considered literate in a more subjective sense; however, the measure would be taken in terms of how well read someone might be or how well informed, or how able to carry out complex tasks that demand the basic tools of literacy. Sometimes the term numeracy is used to indicate how mathematically "literate" someone is.

MAJORING

Majoring is a term used to describe a learning strategy that allows students to select topics of interest to them and to learn about and even teach others about them in ways that they tend to prefer or excel in. Thus, if a student is interested in butterflies, continental drift, medieval architecture, or whatever, he/she is encouraged to pursue this interest and to become an "expert" on the topic. The student is free to use whatever ways to learn are appealing and reasonable to him/her. Thus the student may use construction, a project approach, inquiry, reading, film, and so on. Generally, majoring involves a contractual agreement or some kind of formal understanding between teacher and student(s). This may include the establishment of a time period in which the work will be completed, the scope of the project, etc. In fact, majoring is an example of the Doctrine of Interest, something first developed by the Roman orator Quintilian in the First Century A.D. Quintilian wrote that students learn best when they can choose that which they wish to learn about.

MEANING-CENTERED

A meaning centered approach is an approach to learning which seeks relevance and avoids isolated skills as means of achieving literacy. Meaning-centered instruction focuses on building knowledge and understanding within the natural framework of a child's experience, an important concept with the whole language educational philosophy.

Middle School

The term middle school has been around most of the twentieth century, but it remains greatly misunderstood. In the latter part of the nineteenth century American schools were organized into eight years of grade school and four years of high school. The junior high school evolved from this configuration, leaving six years of elementary school, three of junior high, and three of senior high. The term "junior high school," was thought by many to send an inappropriate signal of a pre-high school catering to students who in fact are at a crucial and significantly different time of life from either that of childhood or young adulthood.

Non-directive Teaching

Non-directive teaching is an approach to learning where the teacher provides minimal structure but helps the students to define their own goals and determine ways to meet those goals. It usually takes the format of a seminar/discussion class where the teacher's role is to listen and seek clarification from the students but not to lead. This is an outgrowth of Carl Rogers' non-directive therapy technique in psychotherapy.

Open Classrooms

Open classrooms represent an educational format that has limited or no formal curriculum, and encourages students to explore and study in areas of their interest in an atmosphere of openness with limited restrictions. Typically, the classrooms look little like traditional classrooms, but rather allow for students to move around to different areas of the rooms which are set up with a variety of learning materials, resources, and activities. Children may work with other children in small groups or individually on projects, readings, etc. The emphasis is on independent learning at a student's own pace. The open classroom idea comes from the *progressive* educational philosophy and was more popular in the 1960s and 1970s than it is today, although such classrooms can still be found.

PROBLEM SOLVING

Problem-solving strategies are those that may be used to apply all previously acquired knowledge and experience to new situations and challenges. Education increasingly focuses on the teaching and reinforcement of individual problem-solving skills as a priority area separate from the imparting of accumulated knowledge.

RECIPROCAL TEACHING

Reciprocal teaching is a technique for improving students' reading comprehension. It involves a four step group teaching/learning process in which students 1) summarize the contents of a passage, 2) ask questions about the main idea of the passage, 3) clarify the difficult aspects of the material, and 4) predict what will happen next. Generally, reciprocal teaching begins as a teacher-centered strategy with the teacher modeling the steps, but the idea is for the center of gravity to shift to the students, creating a peer teaching effect.

REFLECTIVE THINKING

Reflective teaching or practice is an approach used in teaching in which a problem (in teaching or learning) is first set or interpreted in theory, experiences, and understandings, and then a solution to the problem is developed through testing, self-evaluations, and a series of revisions. It is inquiry-oriented and, as the title states, it is reflective in that learners are expected to take the measure of their experience, to consider it thoughtfully, and to reach conclusions about the worth or efficacy of the approach they take. Often, reflective thinking is encouraged in environments where students compare their problem-solving processes with each other's, with those of an expert, or with an ideal model. The origins of reflective thinking as a teaching and learning strategy are found in the works of John Dewey.

Donald Schon has developed a theory of reflection-in-action that requires problem setting (or diagnosis), testing, and belief in personal causation (personal or professional values used in setting the problem, and responsibility for actions taken). Another approach to reflective teaching includes action or reflection through recollections, representation, analysis, and conceptual base for future reference. Donald Cruickshank has developed a series of reflective teaching lessons (RTL) to be used by preservice teacher education majors—in these lessons, the teacher and learner reflect together on the teaching/ learning experience. Reflective teaching is used in clinical supervision and as a part of preservice education in some universities.

SCAFFOLDING

Scaffolding is a term introduced by the psychologist Jerome Bruner to indicate support for someone's learning, especially in *problem solving* and *discovery learning*. Scaffolding usually consists of clues, examples, connections, reminders, encouragement, or anything that might enable a learner to extend his/her thinking about a problem. The idea is to encourage the learner to do his/her own thinking but with a little support, in a way much like the use of training wheels on a bicycle that in time are removed.

SCHEMA THEORY

Schema theory refers to a concept that focuses on the relationship between prior knowledge and comprehension. The theory explains the way in which experiences and related concepts are stored in memory. Schema (schemata, pl.) is the individual's internal explanation of the nature of situations, objects, etc., that are encountered; it is the way knowledge is organized within the brain. These schemata are constantly being altered and/or changed as new knowledge is absorbed.

In reading comprehension, the schemata form the ties between reader and text. With no relatable experience or concepts, a reader would find the understanding of a selection to be most difficult. The importance of a purposeful building of background knowledge through pre-reading activity, structured comprehension follow-through, and experience-based vocabulary development in order to create the cognitive structures is apparent.

SCOPE AND SEQUENCE

Scope and sequence are terms especially associated with curriculum planning. Scope refers to the breadth of coverage within a course of study, for example, U.S. History from Colonial times to the Civil War for 8th grade. Sequence refers to the order in which subjects are to be learned, for example, arithmetic precedes advanced mathematics in most curriculums. Most states and school districts have elaborate guides and charts illustrating the scope and sequence of the curriculum from kindergarten through senior high school.

SELF-ESTEEM

Self-esteem involves the estimation individuals place on their own perceived attributes, capacities, intentions, and behaviors. The related term, "self-concept," is used interchangeably referring to "the composite of ideas, feelings, and attitudes people have about themselves." (Hilgard, E., et. al., 1979. *Introduction to psychology, 7th ed.* New York: Harcourt, Brace, Jovanovich, p. 605). Considerable controversy exists over whether self-esteem contributes to achievement or achievement contributes to self-esteem, or whether self-esteem is even a stable enough construct to be accorded a sense of validity.

SOCIETY-CENTERED CURRICULUM

Society-centered curriculum is one of two major offshoots of the progressive educational movement, the other being child-centered curriculum. The society-centered curriculum is focused on social issues and socially relevant themes. Little emphasis is place upon learning formal academic disciplines in isolation. The curriculum is invariably interdisciplinary. The underlying idea is that curricular experiences should be related to real-world activities and that they should be socially redemptive. Most society-centered activities are group projects where students learn to work together. Among the more notable examples of society-centered curricula are peace education, environmental education, global education, and multi-cultural education.

Socioculturalism

Socioculturalism is a theory of learning and knowledge which postulates that learning is primarily a process of enculturation into a community of practice. Sociocultural learning is often considered to be a type of constructivism, but one which places less emphasis on the individual's interior processes of active cognitive reorganization, as Piaget postulated, and greater emphasis on the social/cultural settings in which learning takes place. Much of the original contribution to socioculturalism can be traced to the work of Russian psychologist Lev. S. Vygotsky, whose ideas about language and thought were developed in the 1930's. Vygotsky theorized that learning takes place most effectively in the learner's zone of proximal development, which is the stage just beyond his/her own ability to learn without expert guidance. Sociocultural theorists emphasize the importance of social interaction with more knowledgeable others, leading many to conclude that apprenticeships and the other practical-oriented activities are indeed valuable learning experiences.

Structure of the Disciplines

The structure of the disciplines theory states that each discipline or body of knowledge has a basic structure composed of 1) its key ideas or concepts, and 2) its methods or process. For example, in anthropology, "culture," "tradition," and "ritual" are concepts or key ideas, and "participant observation," "interviews," and "qualitative assessment" are methods or processes. The idea of the structure of the disciplines was first made educationally prominent by Joseph Schwab and later by Jerome Bruner who used the idea of structure as a cornerstone of his experimental curriculum, "Man: A Course of Study."

SUMMATIVE ASSESSMENT

Summative assessment strategies are those used at the conclusion of the implementation of a new program to determine the overall effectiveness or degree of goal attainment. For example, if a school is implementing a new ninety minute block schedule for the first time, *formative assessment* would take place early in the implementation to provide feedback to the participants on how it is working and what may need modification in order to enhance its chance of success. Summative assessment would be used once the program was in place in its entirety and educational outcomes, such as achievement, attendance, attitudes, etc. would be checked to determine if the program was a success. Summative assessment is sometimes referred to as product assessment because much of the assessment activities are concerned with the final product after full implementation. Data collected is usually quantitative in nature, but may also be qualitative if the program goals are more affective in nature. When the concept of summative assessment is applied to a classroom setting it may be thought of as the final unit test a teacher gives to students to assess the degree which the objective has been reached.

TEACHING

Jean Piaget described teaching as the establishing of environments where students' cognitive structures could emerge and grow. Such a description would match the concept of the teacher as facilitator. An advocate of direct instruction might describe teaching as the act of imparting needed skills, knowledge, and values to learners. But those who hold to either perspective would agree that teaching involves far more than child-minding. Teaching includes planning, organizing, reflecting, acting, reacting, assessing, and above all, continuous problem solving.

TEACHING STRATEGIES

Teaching strategies are the approaches or methods teachers use in order to ensure student learning. Broadly speaking, teaching strategies can be broken down into two large categories: direct and indirect instruction. Direct instruction tends to be teacher-centered and is exemplified by lecture, class discussion, and related means of whole-class instruction. Indirect strategies tend to shift the center of gravity to the student. Examples of indirect instruction include cooperative learning, project methods, discovery learning, and learning centers.

Team Teaching

Team teaching is a system of instructional organization in which two or more teachers work collaboratively to plan, teach, and assess a curriculum to students. It has been noted that the key to effective team teaching is team planning. At the most basic level, teachers plan together but teach separately. A second stage occurs when teachers not only plan together but share instruction, at times teaching together to a combined group. A variant of this is for one teacher to instruct while the other either monitors and helps students or evaluates his/her peer's effectiveness. Team teaching was highly touted in the 1960's, and teams of teachers were given generous training grants by the Ford Foundation. As a fad, it gradually subsided, but its legacy is very much alive, and one finds it at all levels from kindergarten through university.

Triarchic Theory of Intelligence

The Triarchic Theory of Intelligence is Robert Sternberg's theory which suggests that intelligent human behavior consists of three components: 1) thinking strategies or componential intelligence, including planning performance, and knowledge acquisition; 2) problem solving, or experiential intelligence, including insight, creativity, and efficiency; and 3) adaptation, or contextual intelligence, including selecting, reshaping, and maximizing.

Two-Sigma Problem

The two-sigma problem is an educational research finding identified by Benjamin Bloom and his students at the University of Chicago. He and his associates discovered that an average achiever could raise his/her score on criterion measures by two standard deviations (two sigma) if that student were to shift from group learning to tutorial learning, a move from the 50th percentile to about the 98th percentile, which is a substantial achievement. This outcome appeared to hold up across subject matter boundaries, and demonstrated to Bloom and his associates that given proper learning opportunities, the vast majority of students are capable of learning. Recognizing that tutorial instruction for all students is not a realistic possibility, the two sigma problem then becomes one of how to structure learning or how classrooms could be reconfigured to take advantage of the elements of tutorial teaching and learning to achieve the two sigma effect. A variety of options have been tried, with the most promise found in cooperative learning and mastery learning.

WEBBING

Webbing, a metaphor based on a spider's web, is a technique employed in *interdisciplinary* teaching and learning. A webbing is a graphic way of identifying key ideas and connecting them to other key ideas, using major and minor categories. Webbings often begin in *brainstorming* sessions where students suggest possible avenues of exploration and topics connected to an organizing theme. Thus if the organizing theme were "energy," then among the obvious connections might be "solar," "atomic," etc.

WHOLE-TO-PART LEARNING

Whole-to-part learning is an approach to learning approach which is said to appeal to *field dependent/global learning styles,* and important in whole language philosophy. In whole-to-part learning, instruction begins with the "big picture," or in a natural setting. As the opportunity and need arises, students are helped to learn individual skills or content as they are needed in a particular setting and when they become meaningful. An example of whole-to-part learning would be asking students to write a story about something meaningful in their lives or within their realm of experiences. As students reread drafts of their stories, and as the needs arise, the stories can be edited and the various rules of grammar can be taught and used in a meaningful way—the inverse of part-to-whole learning.

ZONE OF PROXIMAL DEVELOPMENT

The zone of proximal development is the stage at which a learner can master new material or some task if given proper support, generally in the form of instruction. The idea of the zone of proximal development, which in a practical sense is teaching someone something at a level just beyond what he/she could master without help, is an idea put forth by the Russian psychologist, Lev Vygotsky. According to Vygotsky, there are certain tasks, problems, etc., that a learner is on the verge of being able to master. They are just beyond his/her independent ability to grasp. A teacher is able to provide the necessary structure for the learner to move into the zone by giving prompts, clues, reminders, or by showing steps. Thus in classroom settings the implication is clear: students should be placed in situations where they must reach cognitively in order to understand, but where instruction from a teacher or more advanced peer is available.

INDEX

academic integrity, 12-14
activities, selection of, 75
Adler, Mortimer, 6
affiliation, 30
analytic learners, 180
Aristotle, 7
assessment of unit, 77
assessment, formative, 174
assessment, summative, 188
astronomy unit, 68-69
Barman, C., 146
Barrera, M., 152
Beane, James, 145
Berney, T.D., 152
Blaydes, J., 158
block scheduling, 20, 163
Bloom, Benjamin, 189-190
Bloom, David, 145
Bloom, Dwila, 146
brainstorming, 164
Brazee, E., 149
broad fields curriculum, 164
Bruner, Jerome, 55
Capelluti, J., 149
Carr, Judy, 150
child-centered curriculum, 164
citizenship, 6
citizenship education, 164-165
collaborative work, 66
colonial encyclopedias, 126
Colonial Times and Revolution, 125-129
Committee of Ten, 31
community, integration of, 37-38
concept map, 165
connections, 50-52
constructionism, 165
constructivism, 166
constructivist theory, 16-18
cooperative learning, 82-86, 166-167
core curriculum, 20, 167-168
Cotton, Kathleen, 20, 25
critical thinking, 168-170
cross-age tutoring, 175
Cruickshank, Donald, 185
curricula, comparisons of traditional and experiential, 49
curriculum, definition, 171-172
curriculum, project-based, 64-68
data collection, 67-68
Deutsch, Morton, 181
Dewey, John, 15-16, 59
Dionisio, Marie, 146
direct instruction, 172-173
discovery learning , 29, 173
discovery, steps of, 39
Drake, Susan, 156
Drucker, Peter, 55
Edison, Thomas, 43
effective schools, 20
Eight Year Study, 19
Eliot, Charles, 31
face-to-face interaction, 181
Fagan, E.R., 151
field dependent, 191
Five, Cora Lee, 146
fragmented learning, 8-10
Fredericks, A., 157
friendship, 30
Gamberg, Ruth, 152
Gardner, Howard, 180
Gardner, John, 47
global learners, 180, 191

Gogol, Nikolai, 53
Goodlad, John, 10
Great Books, 6
group investigation, 84-86
group investigation, planning, 85-86
Hollingsworth, Patricia, 149
Humanitas, 19
Hutchins, Robert, 48
illumination, 39, 42-43
Immigration unit, 132-136
incubation, 39, 41-42
individual accountability, 181
information revolution, 63
inquiry, 44-47
interdisciplinary studies, 174-176
interdisciplinary teams, 81
interdisciplinary, arguments for and against, 23-24
interest, definition, 176-177
interest, doctrine of, 182
interest, student, 62
intuitive learners, 180
IQ tests, 180
Jacobs, Heidi H., 148, 151
Jenkins, John, 156
jigsaw strategy, 177
Johnson, David, 167, 181
Johnson, Judy, 149
Johnson, P., 148
Johnson, Roger, 167, 181
Joplin Plan, 177
Journeys of Discovery, 13, 36, 38, 117-124
Kilpatrick, William, 15
knowledge explosion, 3
knowledge, application of, 61
Lafer, Stephen, 158
Lake, Kathy, 18
leadership, 38
learning centers, 178
learning emphasis, 54-55
learning styles, 178-181
learning together, 181
learning, definition, 177-178
learning, self-directed, 69
Lee, V.E., 21, 26
Levy, Steven, 65
literacy, 181-182
Long, R., 158
majoring, 182
Man: A Course of Study, 187
Manning, G., 158
Manning, M., 158
marine life theme, 74, 76
Mason, T.C., 24, 26
Maurer, Richard, 148
meaning centered learning, 182-183
meaningfulness, 49-50
Meinbach, A., 157
middle school, definition, 183
motivation, 52
non-directive teaching, 183
nondisciplinary, 18
open classrooms, 183-184
Piaget, Jean, 16, 48
planning units, 80
planning web, 78-79
positive interdependence, 181
preparation, 39-41
problem solving, 51, 184
progressive education, 15, 19-20
project approach, 59-61
project structure, 66
projects, 7-8
Quintilian, 182
Rain Forests unit, 93
reciprocal teaching, 184
reflective thinking, 85, 184
resources, adequacy of, 67
Rogers, Carl, 183
Rothlein, L., 157
Rousseau, Jean-Jacques, 50
Rusch, J., 146

Russian schools, 22
scaffolding, 185
schema theory, 185-186
Scheuerman, Richard, 152
Schon, Donald, 185
school-to-life connections, 62
Schwab, Joseph, 55
scope and sequence, 186
Seely, Amy, 150
selective coverage, 6-7
self-esteem, 186
Sharan, S., 84
Sharan, Y., 84
Slavin, Robert, 82-84
Smith, J.B., 21, 26
social living, 20
society-centered curriculum, 186-187
socioculturism, 187
spiral curriculum, 14-15
stages of group investigation, 84
Sternberg, Robert, 189
Stevenson, Chris, 150
STREAMS, 106-112
structure of the disciplines, 187
students, integration of, 37
Tanner, Daniel, 156
Tchudi, Stephen, 158
teachers, integration of, 37
teaching strategies, 188-189
teaching, definition, 188
team teaching, 77-82, 189
tertiary materials, 47
The Core Teacher, 157
themes, 69-71
themes selection, 71
thinking skills, 82
To Kill a Mockingbird, 131
topic selection, 64, 85
triarchic theory of intelligence, 189
two-sigma problem, 189-190
unit guidelines, 72
Vars, Gordon, 26, 151
verification, 39, 43-44
visual map, 73
Vygotsky, Lev, 16-17, 187
Walker, Decker, 20
Wallas, Graham, 39
webbing, 190
whole-to-part learning, 190-191
writing outcomes, 72-73
zone of proximal development, 17, 191